THE MYSTERY OF
BLOODY MARY
A GHOSTLY GRAPHIC

by Nel Yomtov

illustrated by Maurizio Campidelli

CAPSTONE PRESS
a capstone imprint

Published by Capstone Press, an imprint of Capstone
1710 Roe Crest Drive, North Mankato, Minnesota 56003
capstonepub.com

Library of Congress Cataloging-in-Publication Data
Names: Yomtov, Nel, author. | Campidelli, Maurizio, 1962– illustrator.
Title: The mystery of Bloody Mary : a ghostly graphic / by Nel Yomtov;
illustrated by Maurizio Campidelli.
Description: North Mankato, Minnesota : Capstone Press, an imprint of Capstone,
[2024] | Series: Ghostly graphics | Includes bibliographical references. | Audience:
Ages 9 to 11 | Audience: Grades 4–6 | Summary: "Mirror, mirror on the wall, who's
the scariest spirit of them all? Bloody Mary—the gruesome ghost who haunts those
who dare to play a ghoulish game. It is said that repeating her name in front of a
looking glass will bring this blood-soaked specter to your bathroom mirror! Who
could Bloody Mary be? And what happens when she is called forth from the great
beyond? Young readers will find out in this easy-to-read ghostly graphic novel that
will send shivers down their spines!"—Provided by publisher.
Identifiers: LCCN 2022048175 (print) | LCCN 2022048176 (ebook) |
ISBN 9781669050605 (hardcover) | ISBN 9781669071389 (paperback) |
ISBN 9781669050568 (pdf) | ISBN 9781669050582 (kindle edition) |
ISBN 9781669050599 (epub)
Subjects: LCSH: Bloody Mary (Legendary character)—Comic books,
strips, etc. | Mirrors—Comic books, strips, etc. | Ghosts—Comic books,
strips, etc. | Graphic novels.
Classification: LCC GR75.B56 Y66 2024 (print) | LCC GR75.B56 (ebook)
| DDC 398.25—dc23/eng/20221213
LC record available at https://lccn.loc.gov/2022048175
LC ebook record available at https://lccn.loc.gov/2022048176

Editorial Credits
Editor: Christopher Harbo; Designer: Sarah Bennett;
Production Specialist: Katy LaVigne

All internet sites appearing in back matter were available
and accurate when this book was sent to press.

Printed and bound in the USA. 5425

TABLE OF CONTENTS

INTRODUCTION

MIRROR, MIRROR ON THE WALL

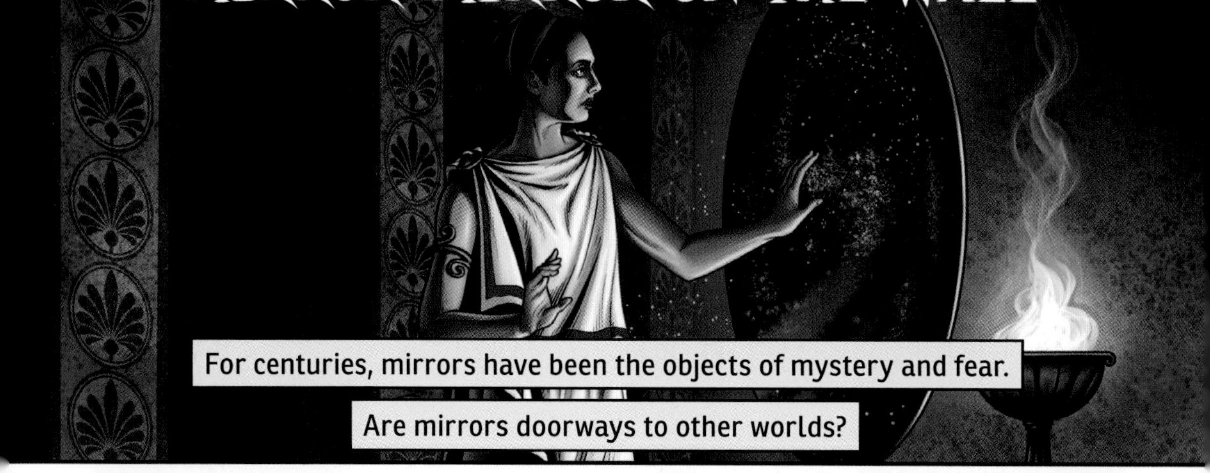
For centuries, mirrors have been the objects of mystery and fear.
Are mirrors doorways to other worlds?

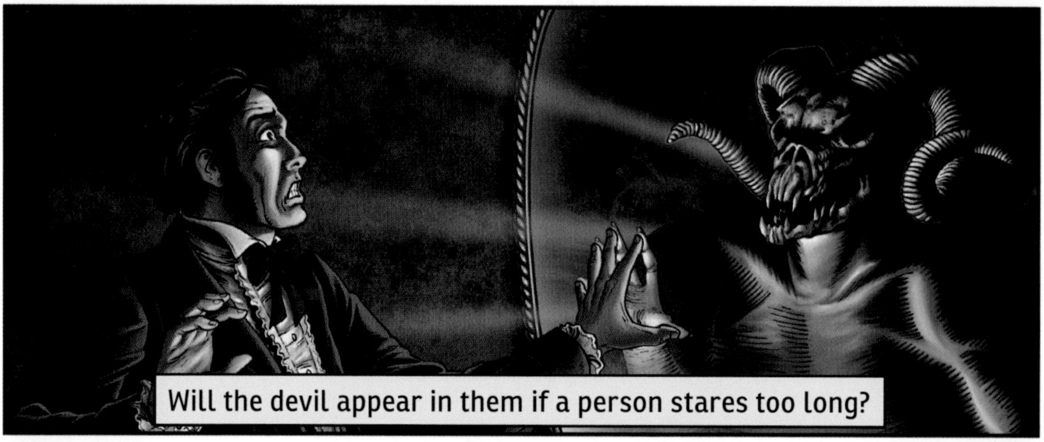
Will the devil appear in them if a person stares too long?

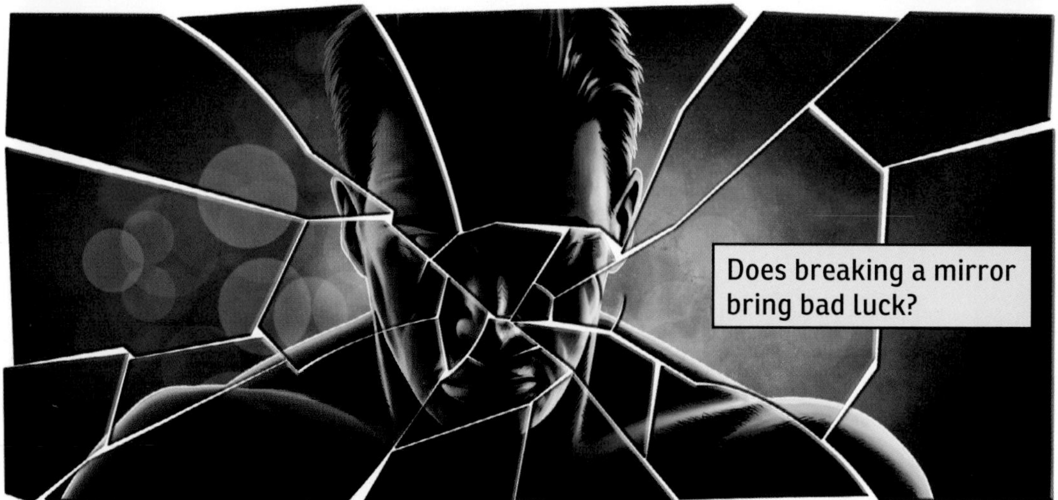
Does breaking a mirror bring bad luck?

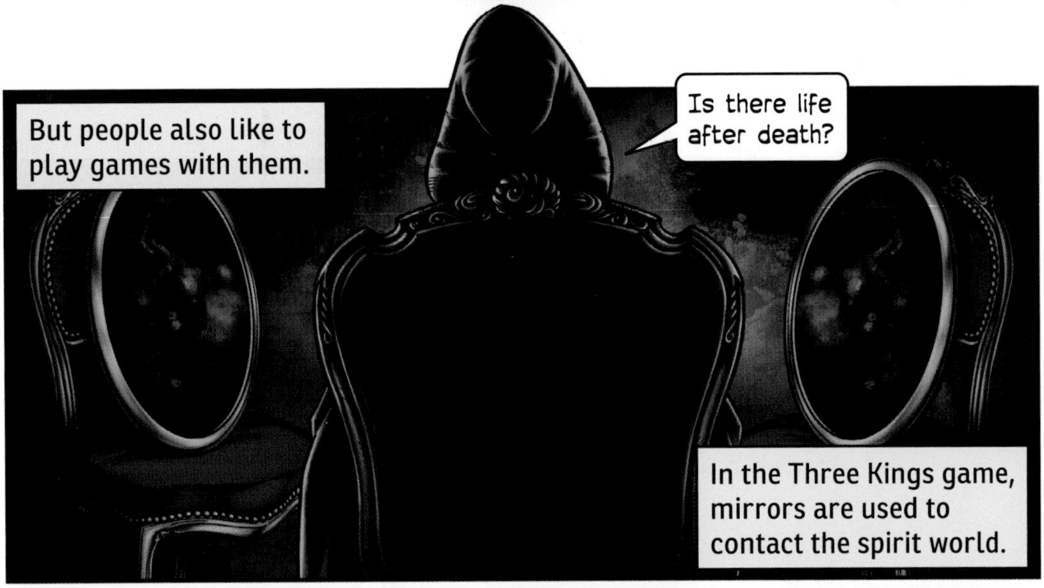
But people also like to play games with them.
Is there life after death?
In the Three Kings game, mirrors are used to contact the spirit world.

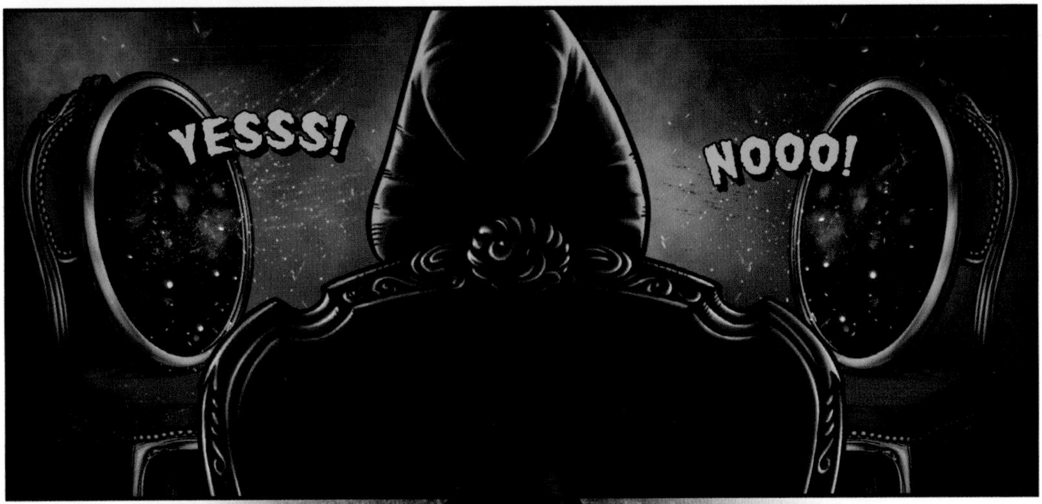
YESSS!
NOOO!

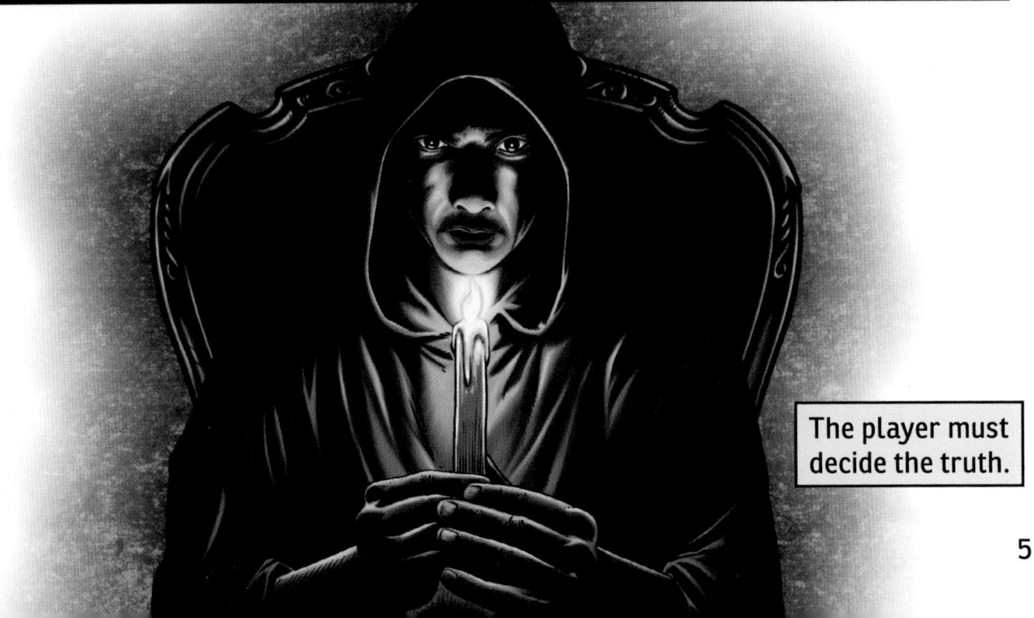
The player must decide the truth.

In Lady Spades, players ask for a wish to be granted.

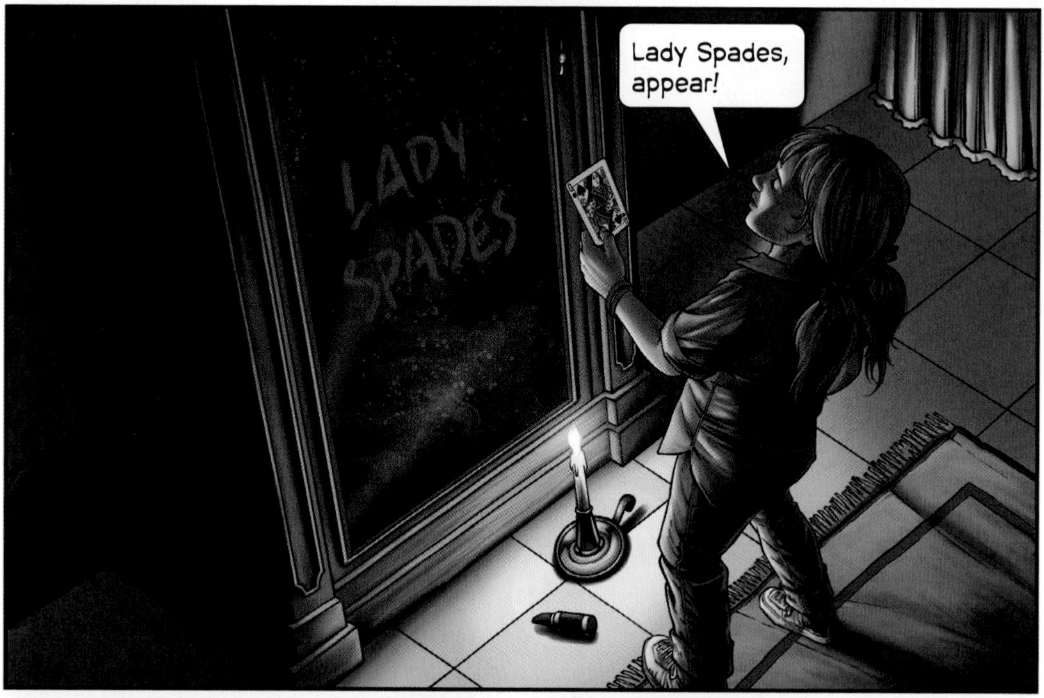
Lady Spades, appear!
LADY SPADES

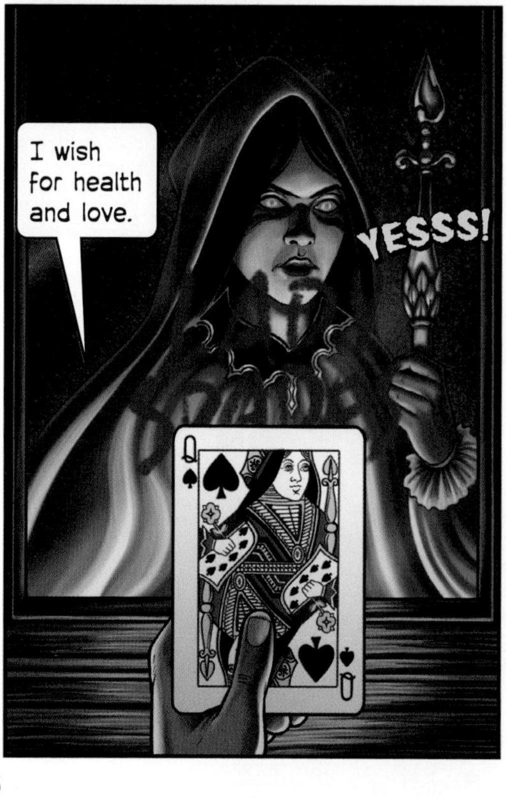
I wish for health and love.
YESSS!

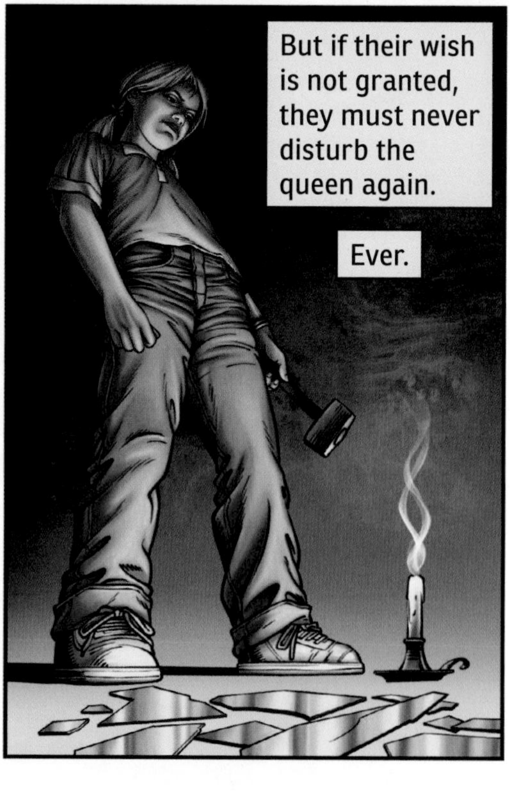
But if their wish is not granted, they must never disturb the queen again.
Ever.

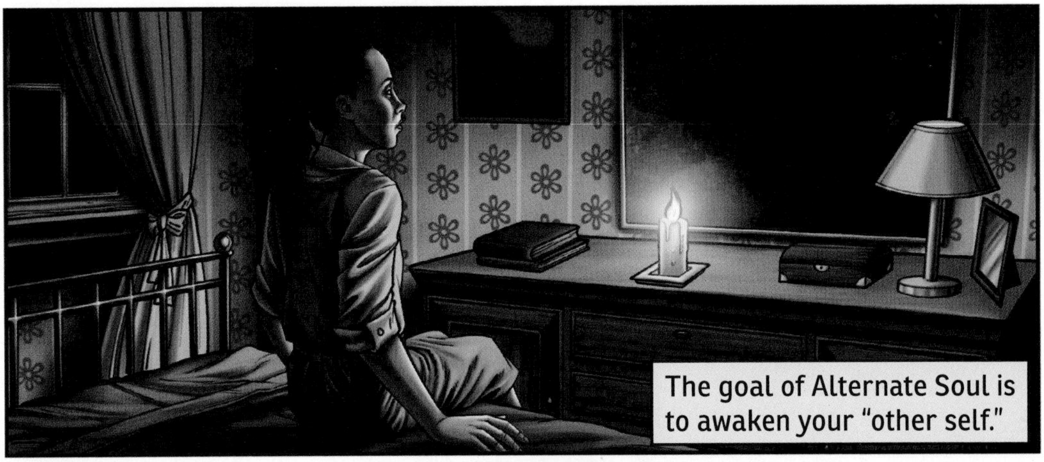
The goal of Alternate Soul is to awaken your "other self."

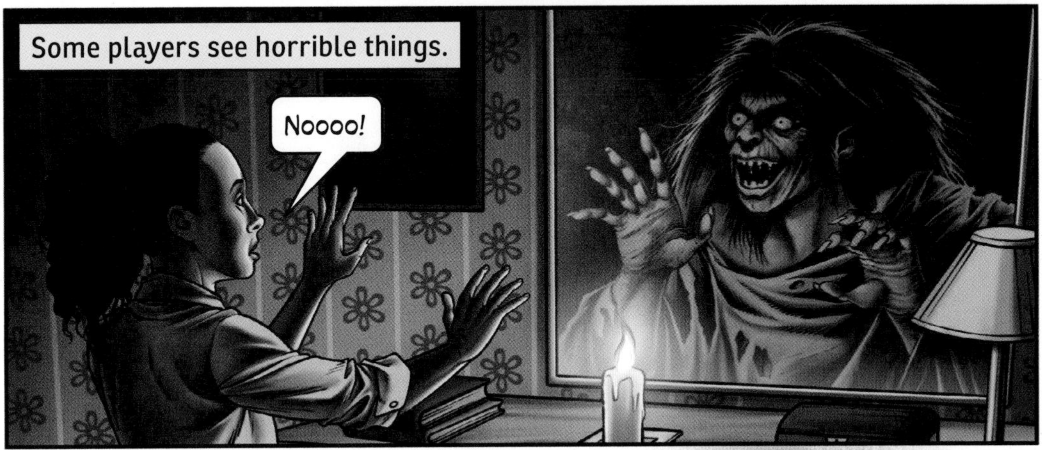
Some players see horrible things.
Noooo!

But the scariest mirror game of all reveals history's most evil ghoul . . .

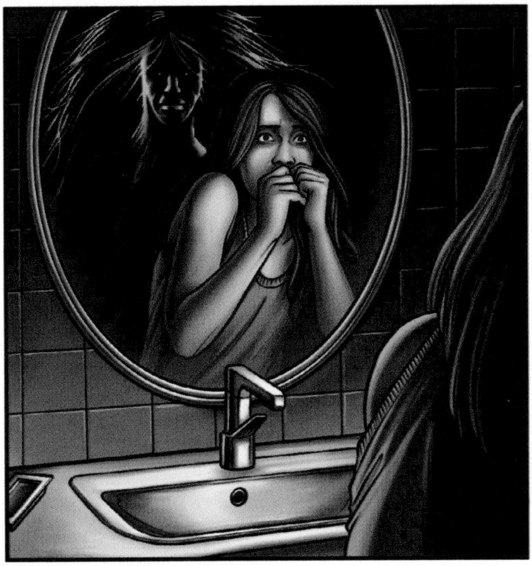

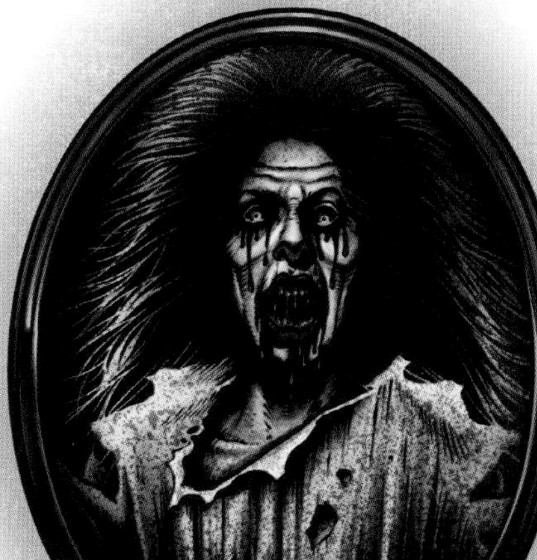

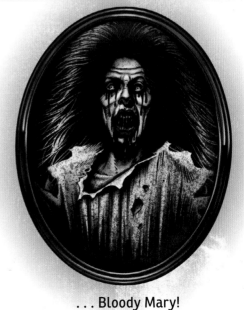

. . . Bloody Mary!

CHAPTER 1

BLOODY MARY: WHERE EVIL LURKS

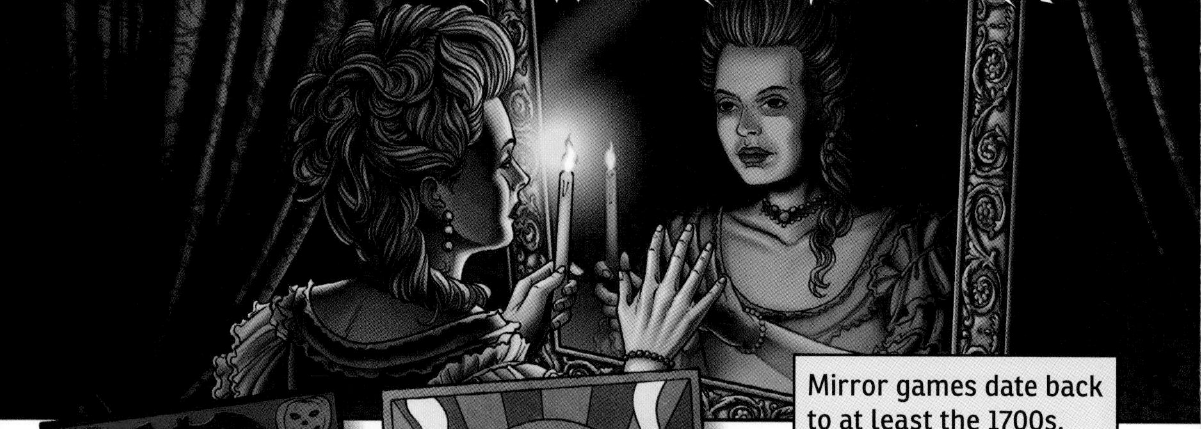
Mirror games date back to at least the 1700s.

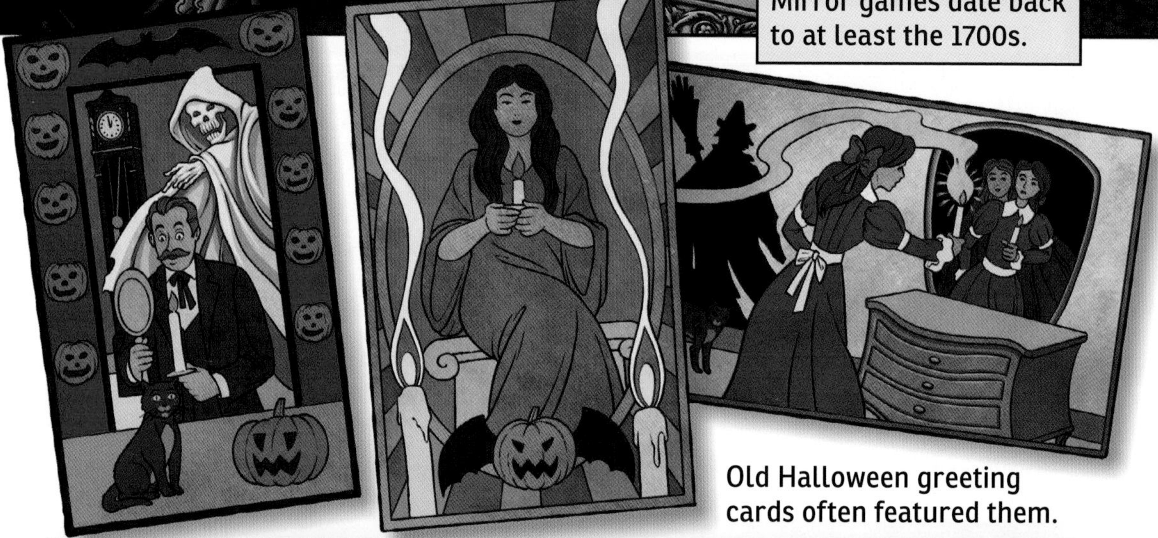

Old Halloween greeting cards often featured them.

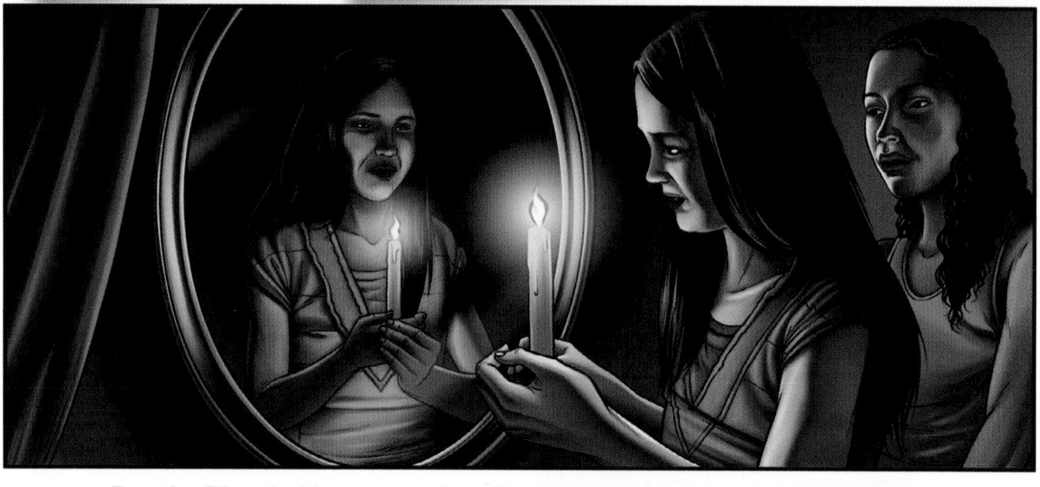

But the Bloody Mary game has been around only since the 1970s.

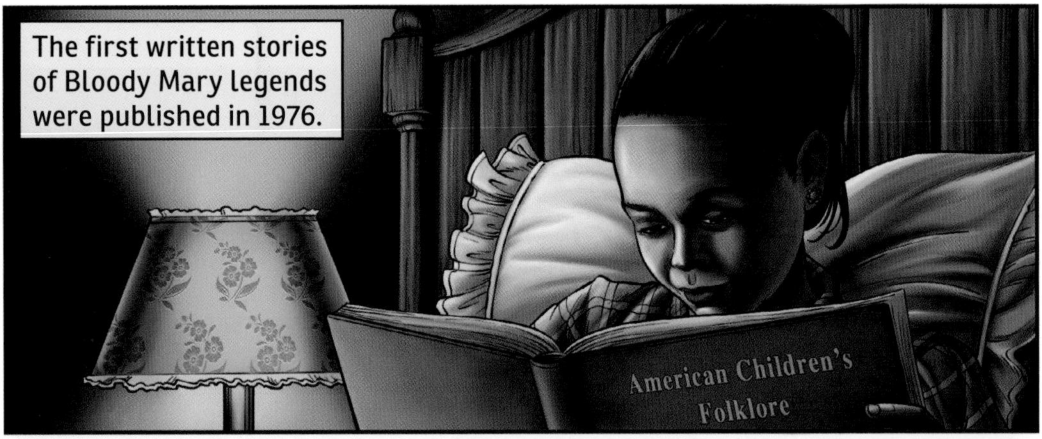
The first written stories of Bloody Mary legends were published in 1976.
American Children's Folklore

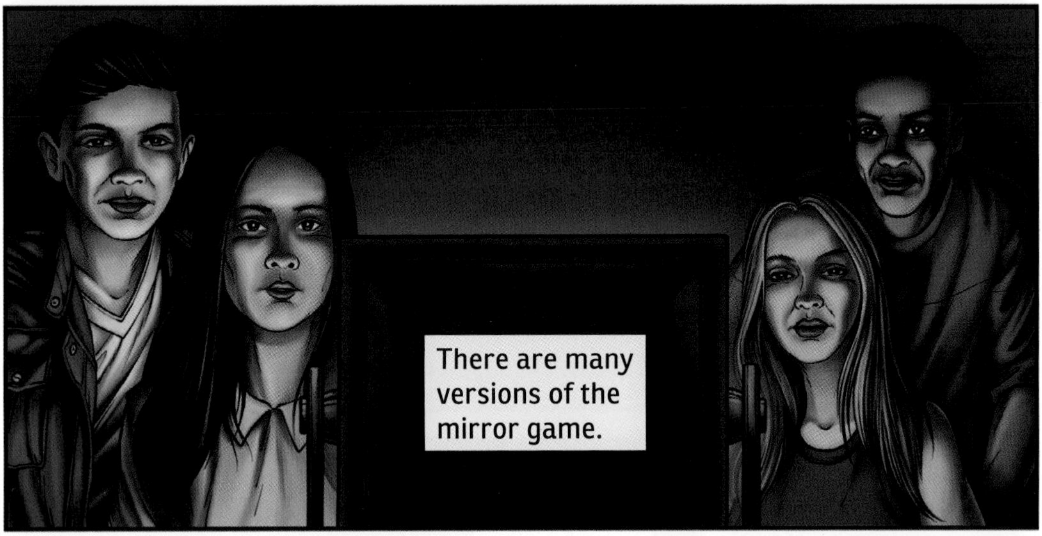
There are many versions of the mirror game.

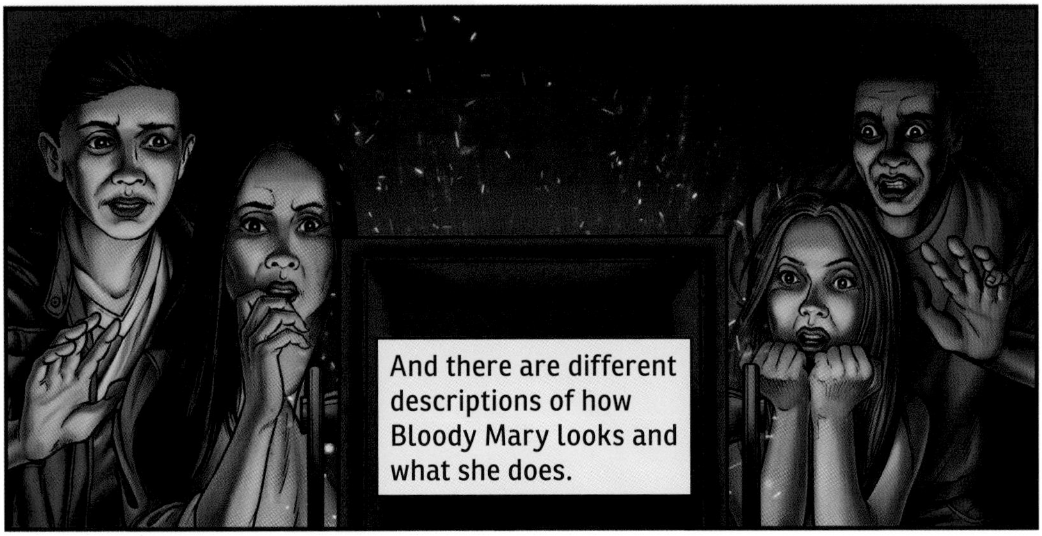
And there are different descriptions of how Bloody Mary looks and what she does.

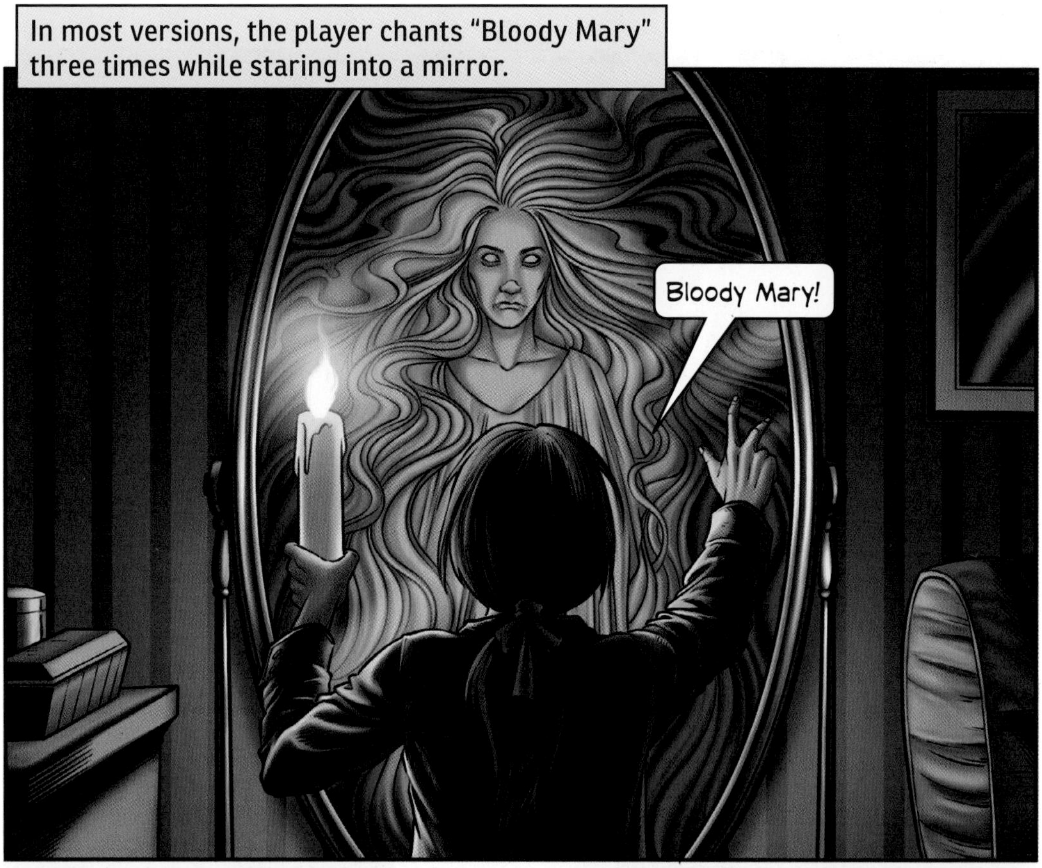
In most versions, the player chants "Bloody Mary" three times while staring into a mirror.
Bloody Mary!

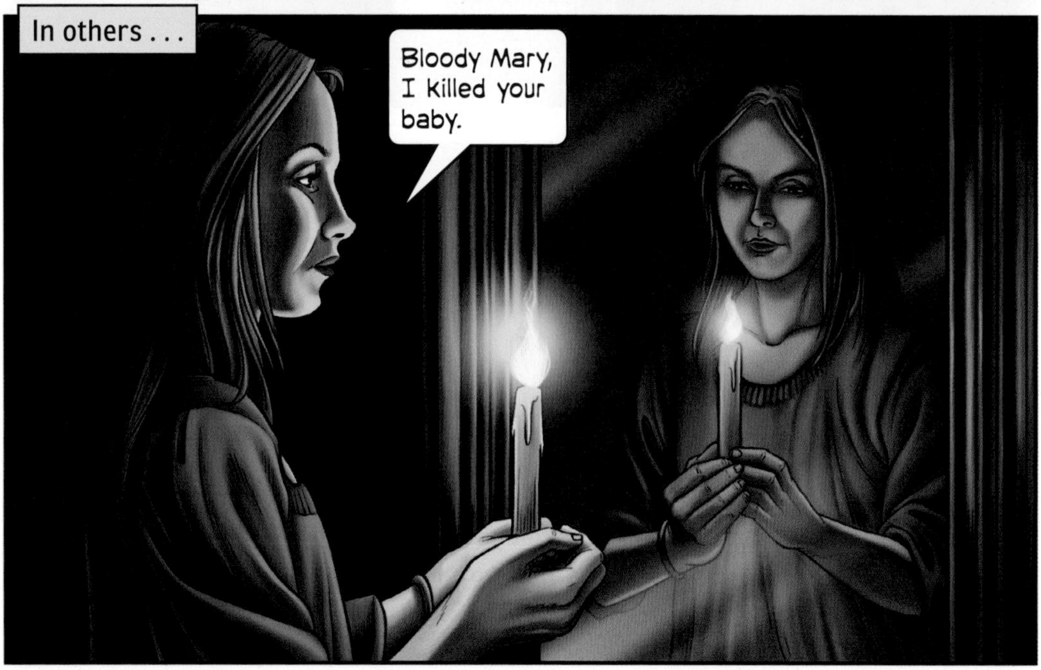
In others . . .
Bloody Mary, I killed your baby.

Some players splash water on the mirror to help call upon Bloody Mary.

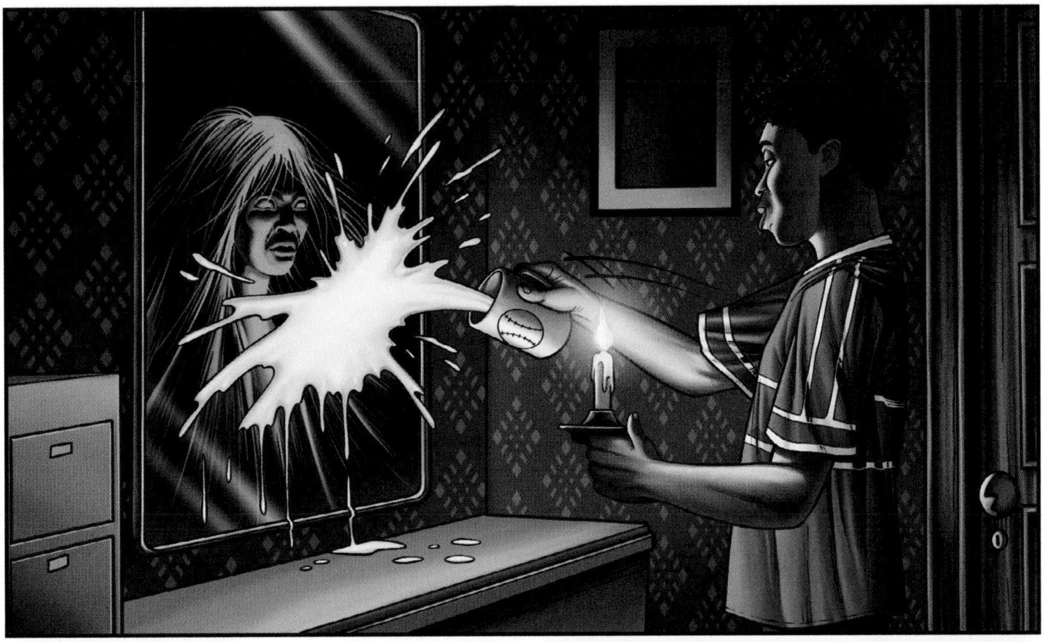

Some spin in a circle as they chant.

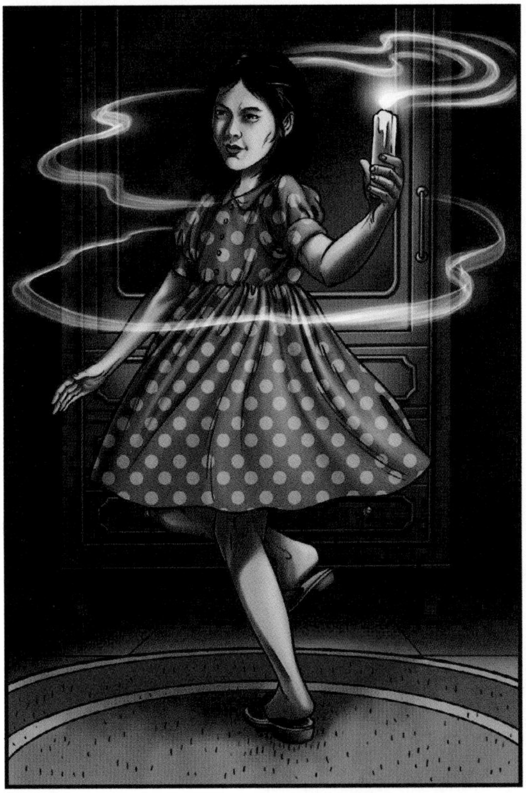

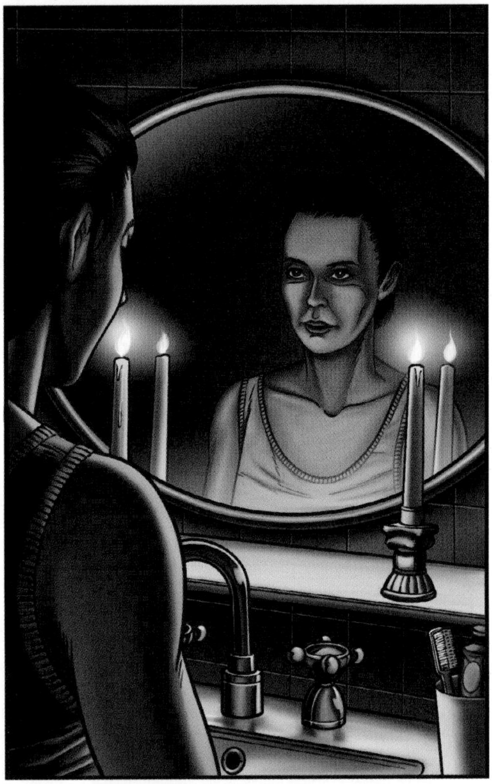

And most play the game in bathrooms.

Bloody Mary usually appears as a ghost or even a dead body.

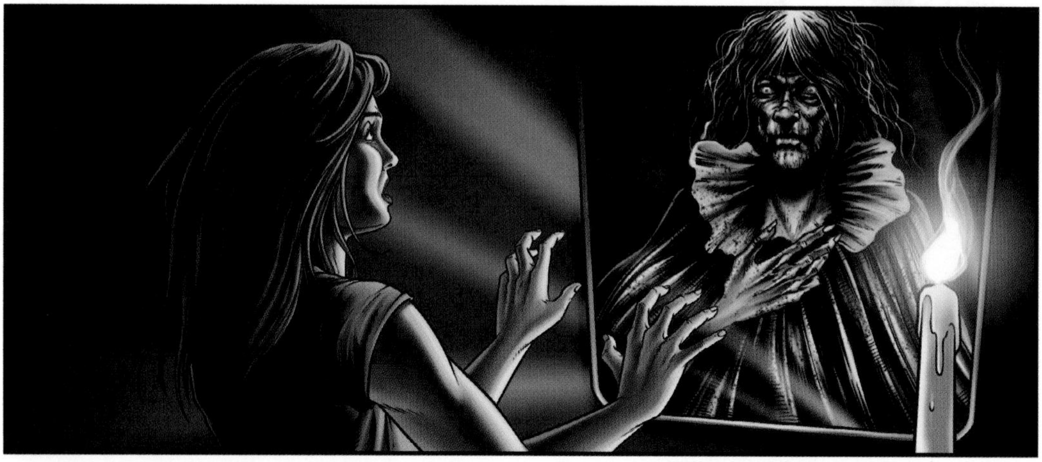

She is always dripping in blood.

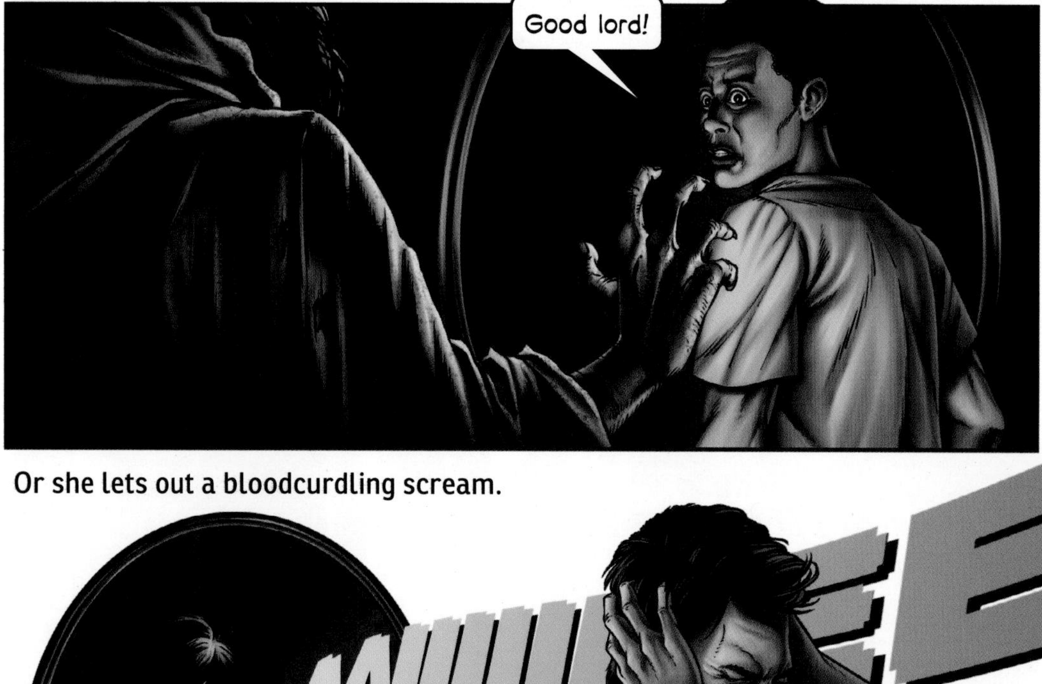
Good lord!

Or she lets out a bloodcurdling scream.

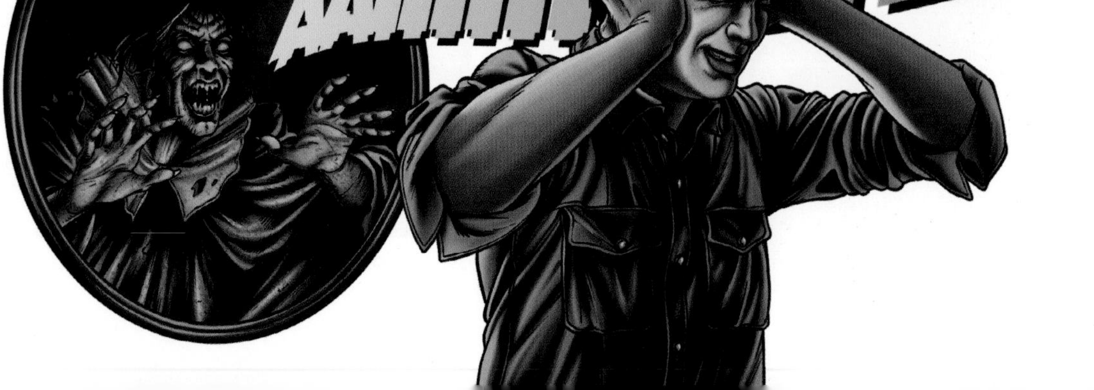
AAIIIIIIEE

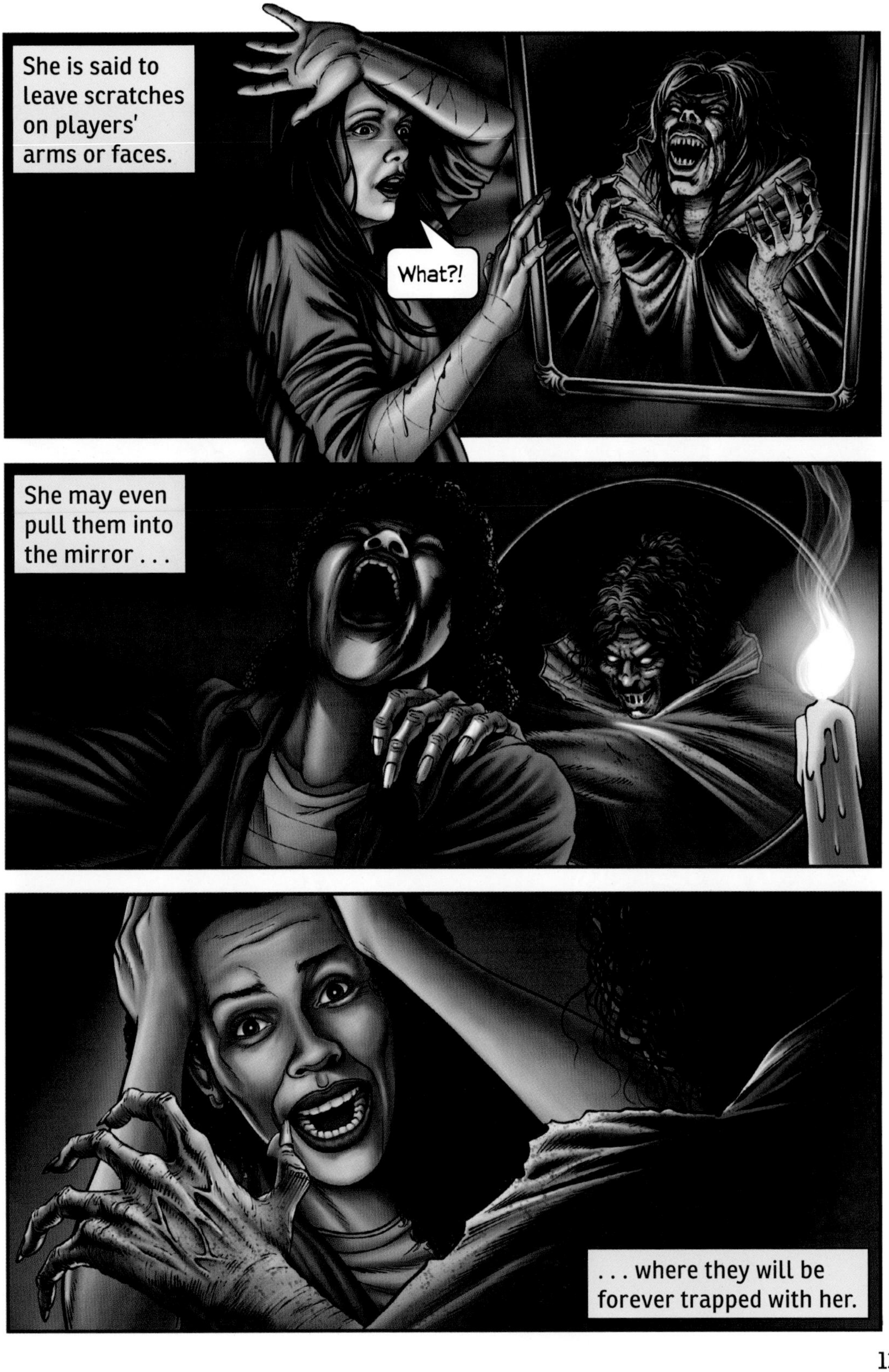
She is said to leave scratches on players' arms or faces.
What?!
She may even pull them into the mirror . . .
. . . where they will be forever trapped with her.

Sometimes Bloody Mary escapes the mirror to steal young souls.

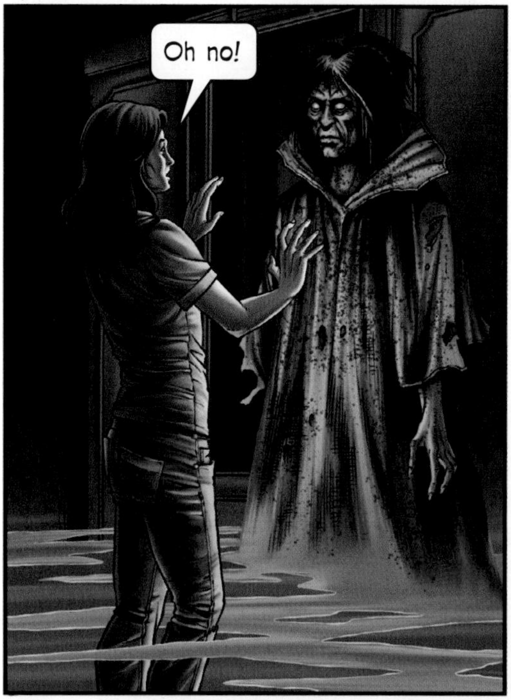
Oh no!

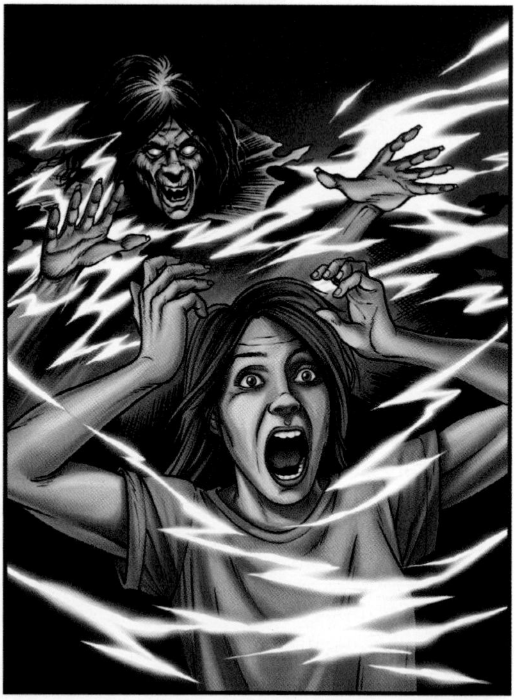

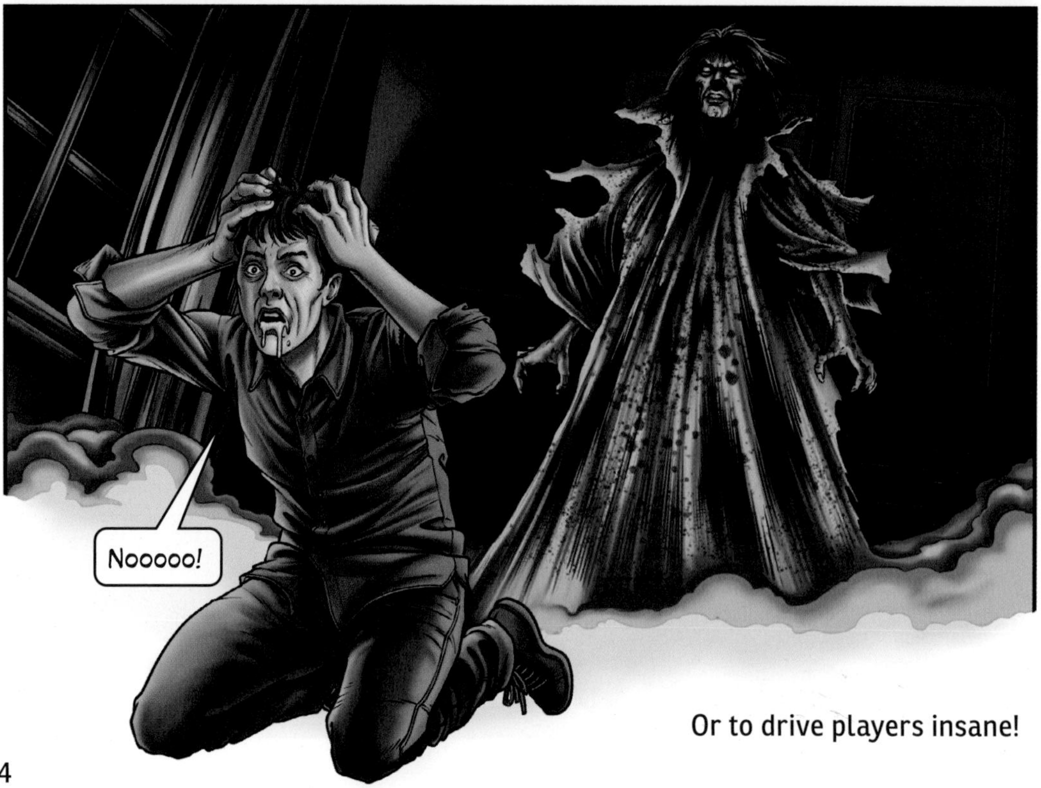
Nooooo!

Or to drive players insane!

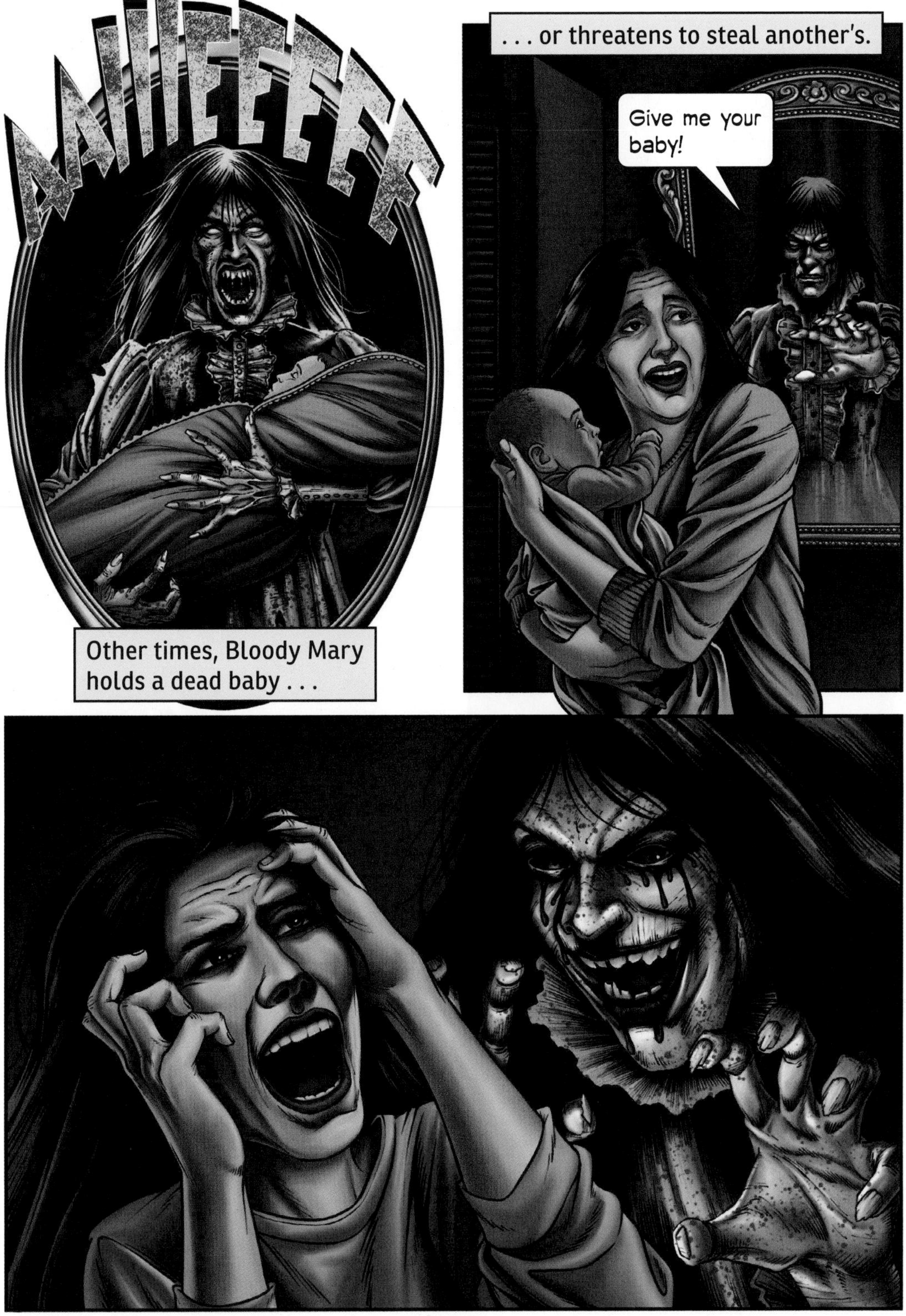
AAIIEEEEE
Other times, Bloody Mary holds a dead baby . . .
. . . or threatens to steal another's.
Give me your baby!

No matter what, be warned. She is evil, dangerous, and deadly.

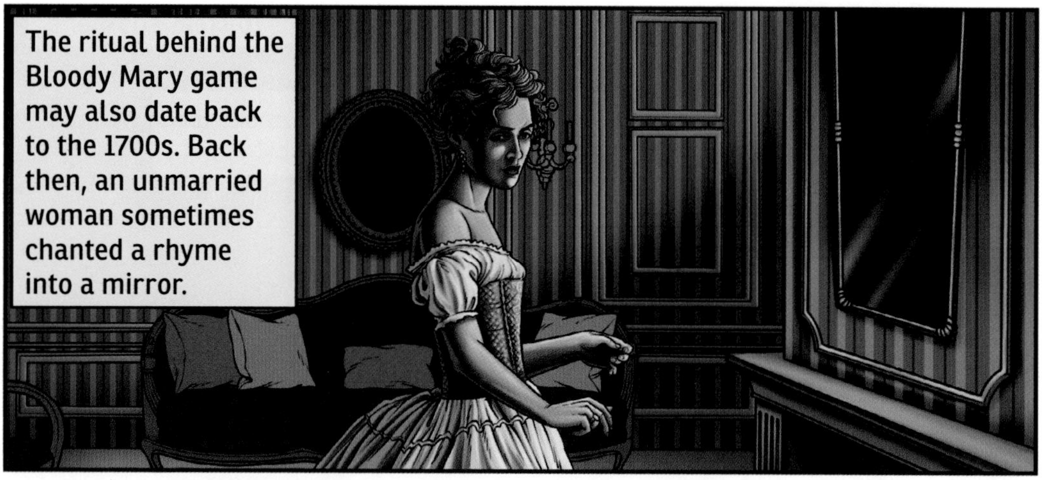
The ritual behind the Bloody Mary game may also date back to the 1700s. Back then, an unmarried woman sometimes chanted a rhyme into a mirror.

Then she looked to see the face of her future husband.

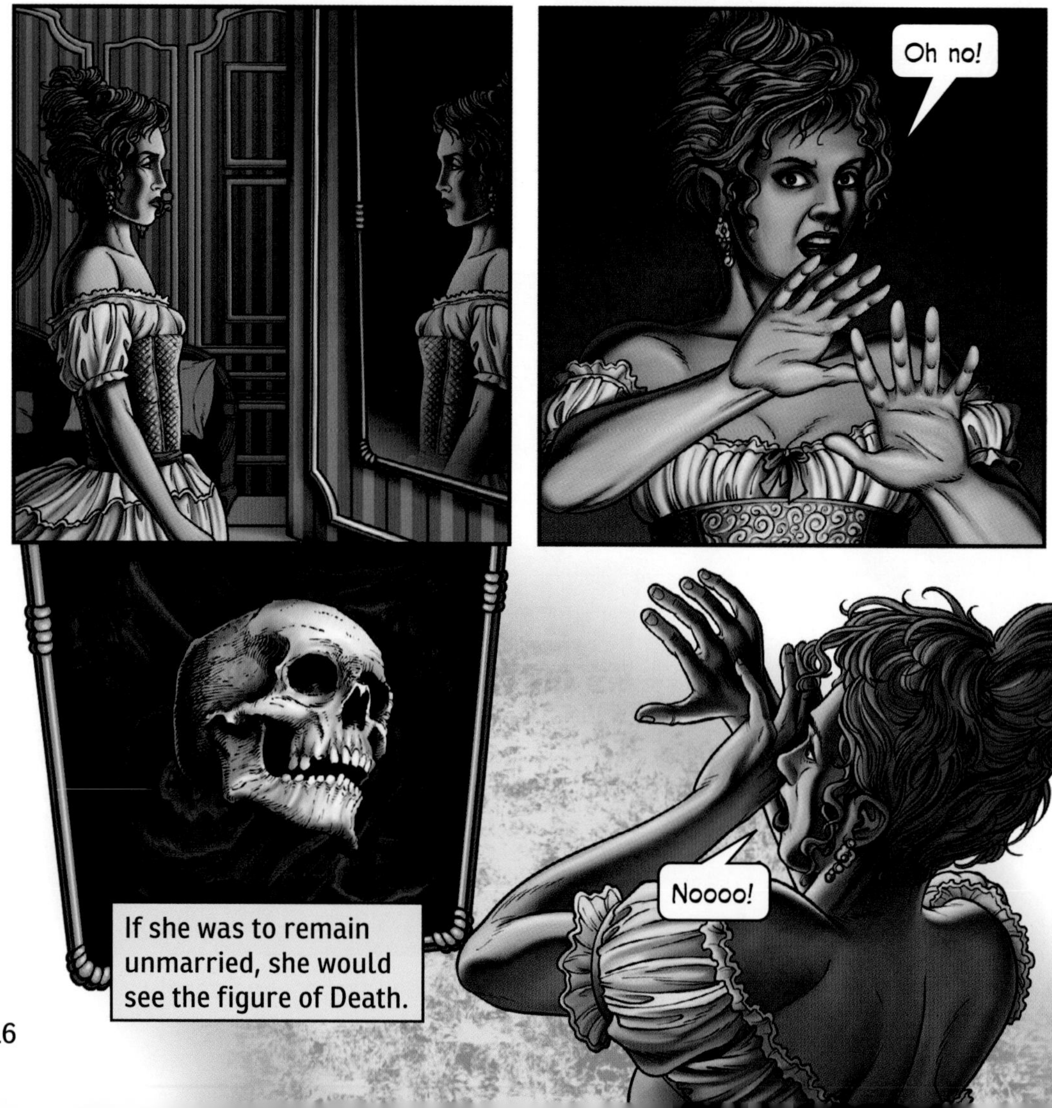
Oh no!
If she was to remain unmarried, she would see the figure of Death.
Noooo!

In another ritual . . .

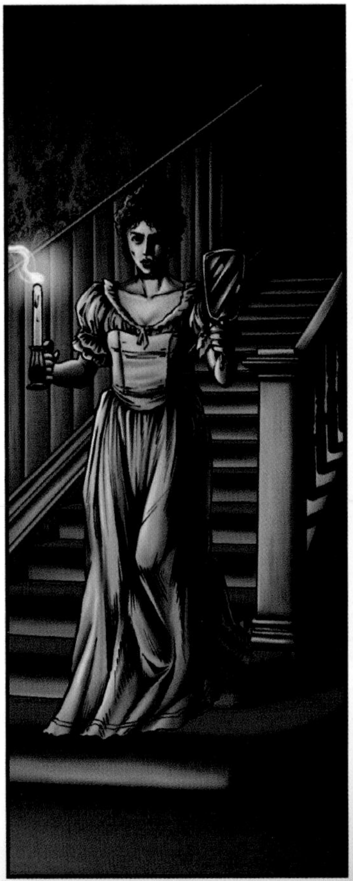

. . . the skull meant the woman would . . .

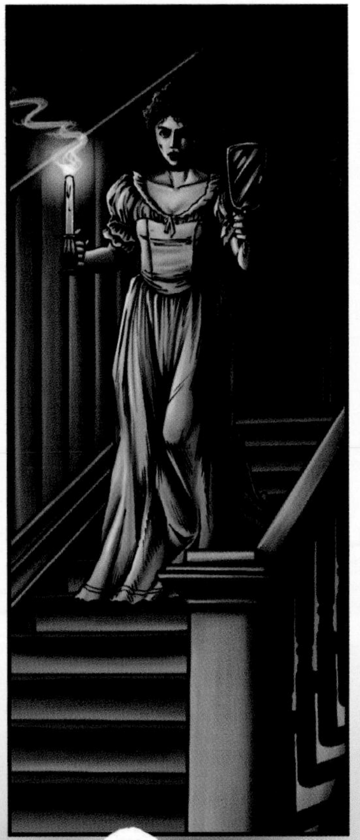

. . . die before she could be married.

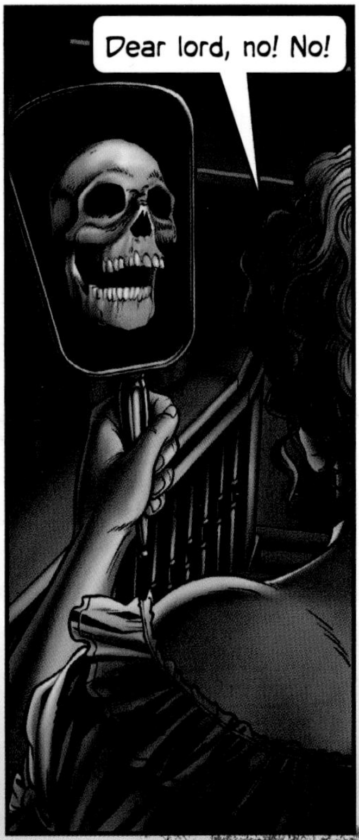
Dear lord, no! No!

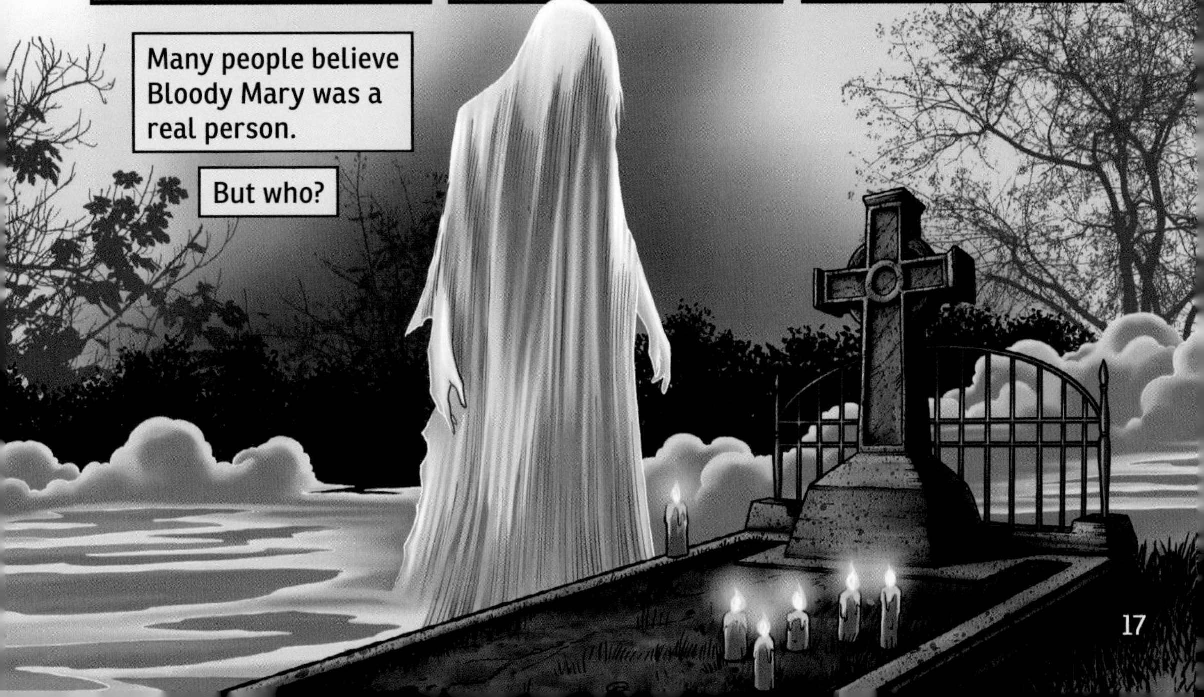
Many people believe Bloody Mary was a real person.
But who?

CHAPTER 2

HISTORY'S REAL-LIFE BLOODY MARY?

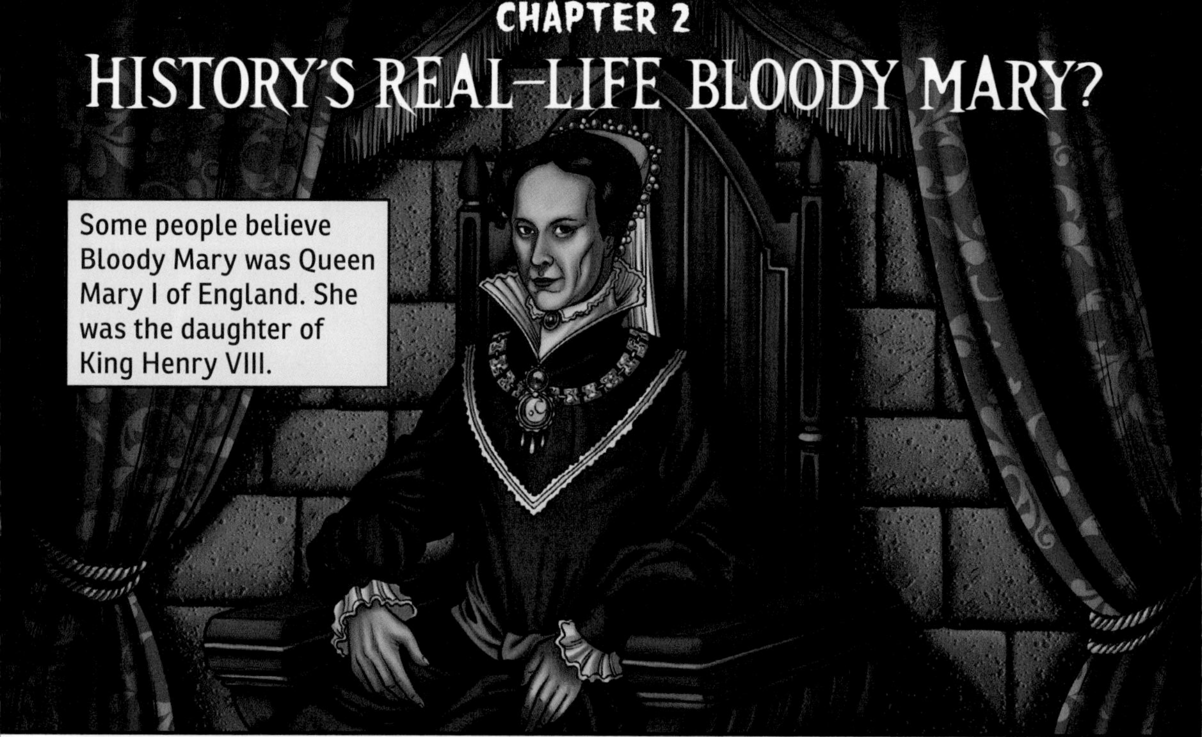
Some people believe Bloody Mary was Queen Mary I of England. She was the daughter of King Henry VIII.

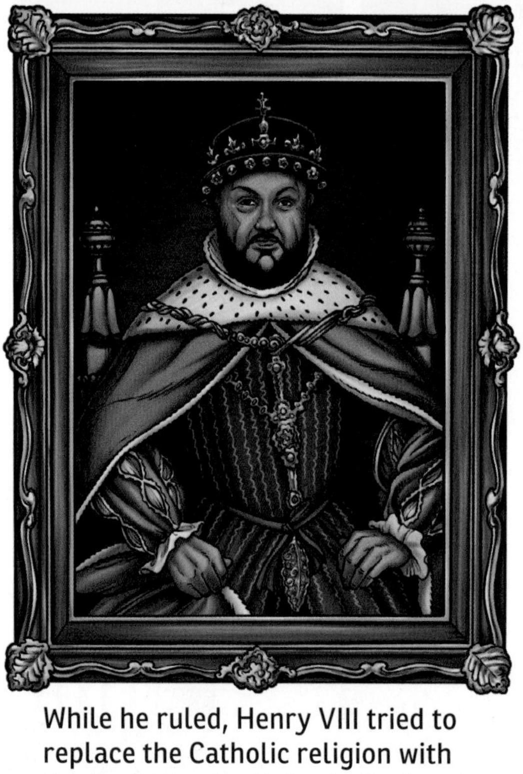

While he ruled, Henry VIII tried to replace the Catholic religion with the Protestant religion in England.

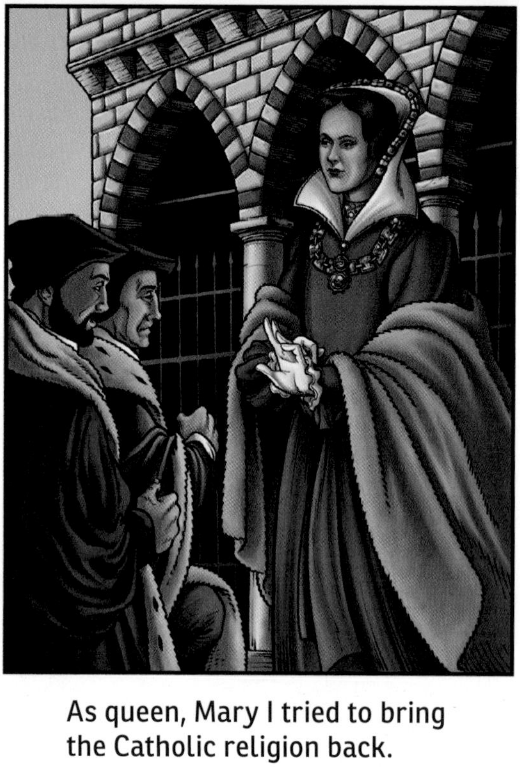

As queen, Mary I tried to bring the Catholic religion back.

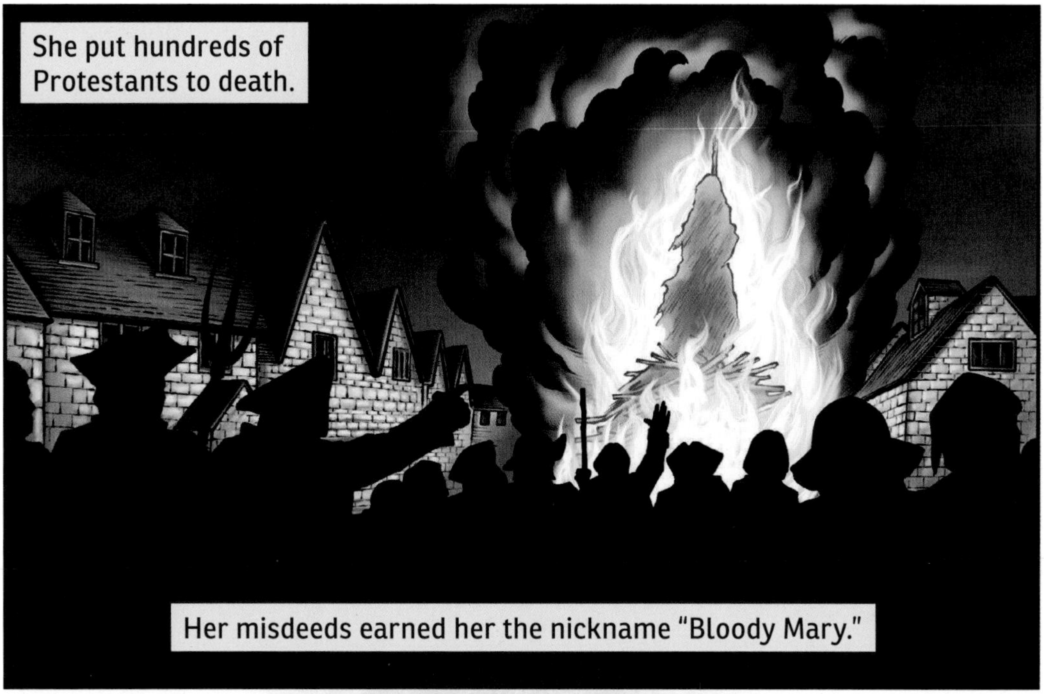
She put hundreds of Protestants to death.
Her misdeeds earned her the nickname "Bloody Mary."

Mary I died at age 42 in 1558.

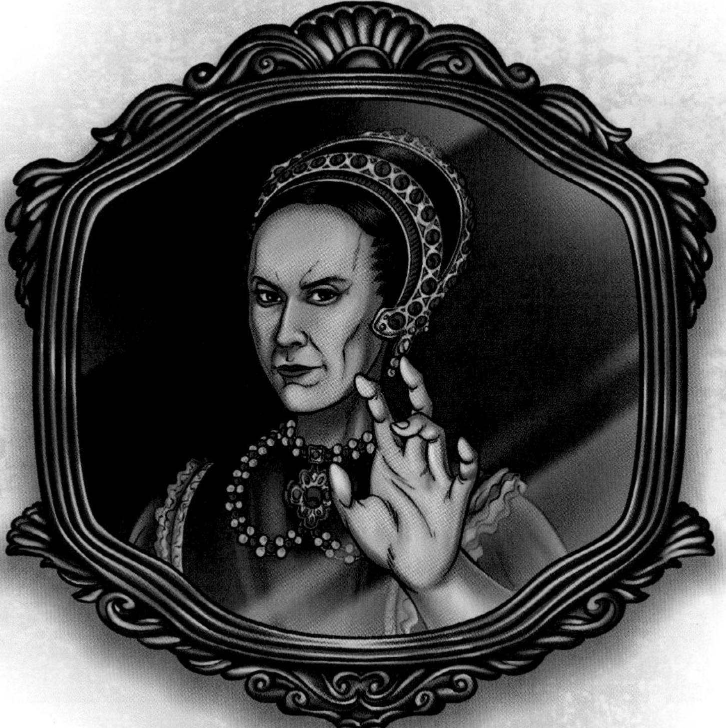

Legend claims she haunts the mirrors of young girls who call out to her.

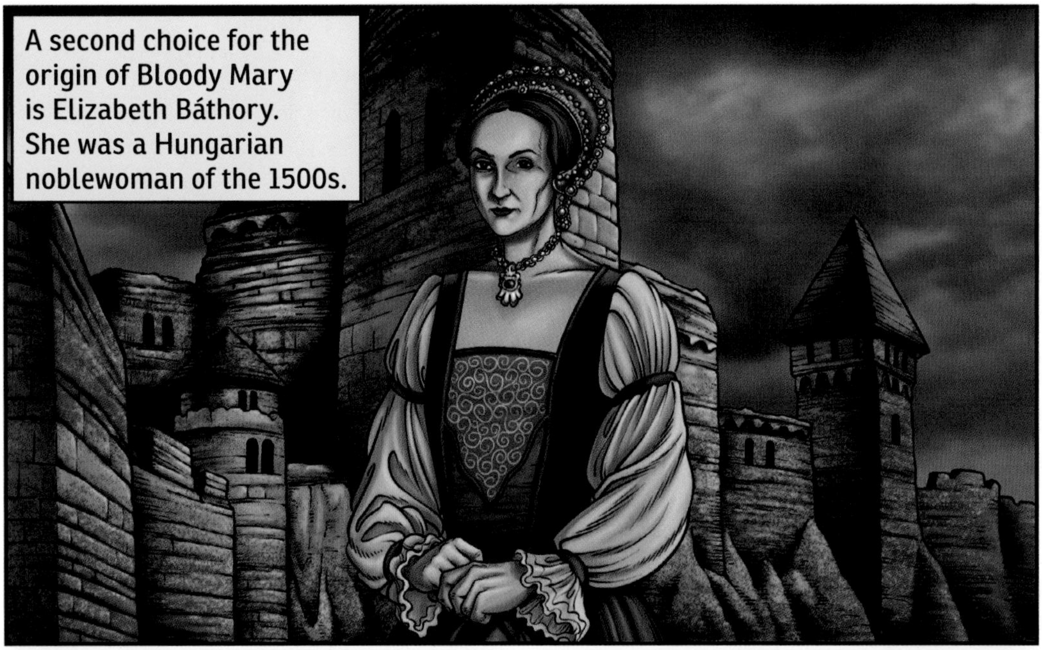
A second choice for the origin of Bloody Mary is Elizabeth Báthory. She was a Hungarian noblewoman of the 1500s.

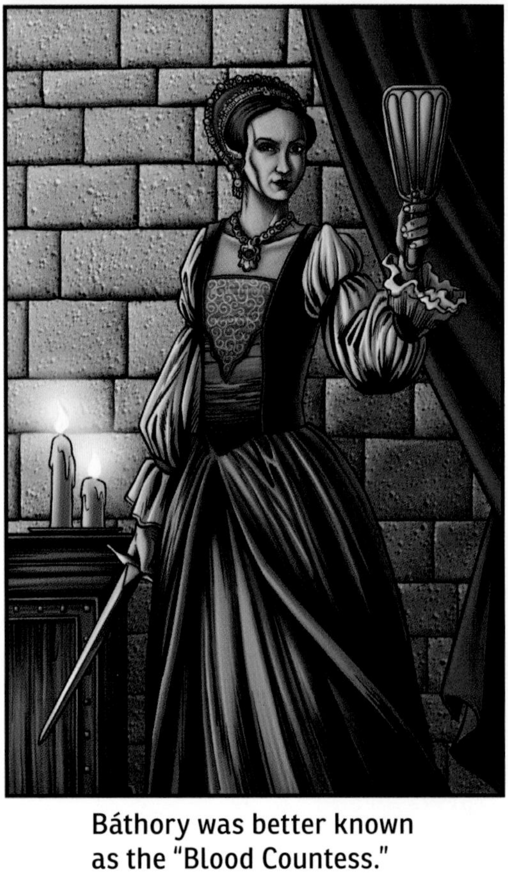

Báthory was better known as the "Blood Countess."

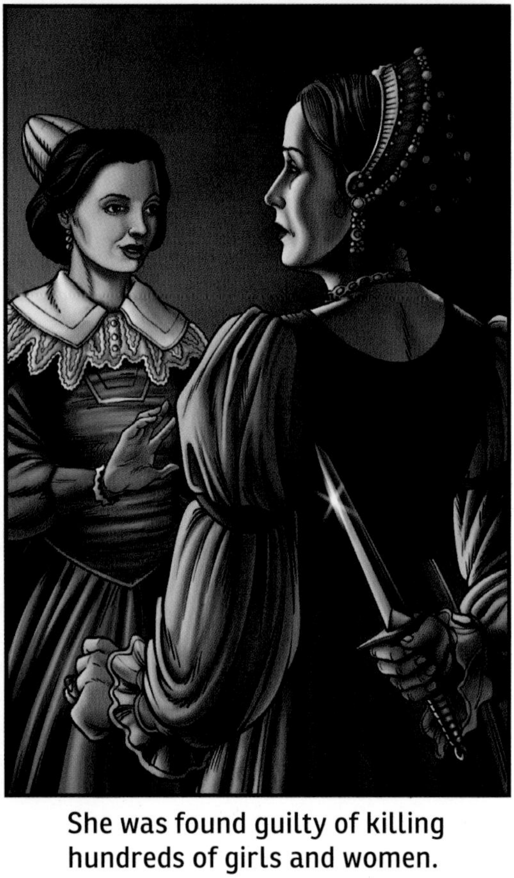

She was found guilty of killing hundreds of girls and women.

It is said she bathed in their blood
to try to remain forever young.

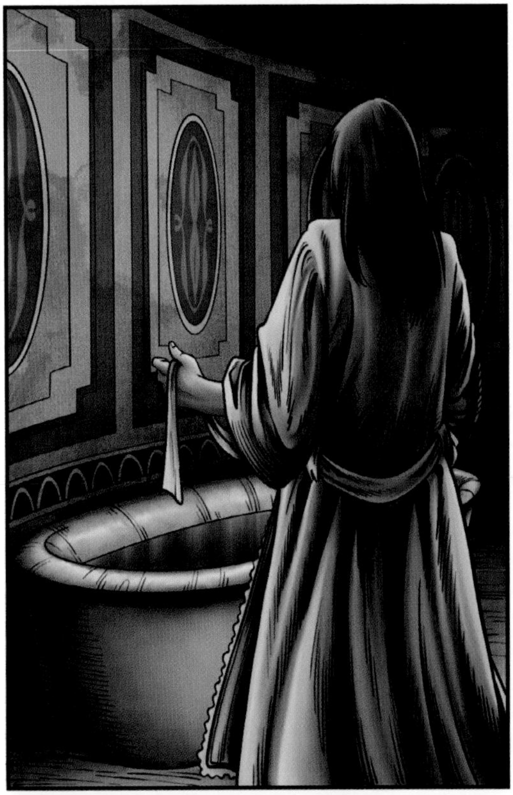

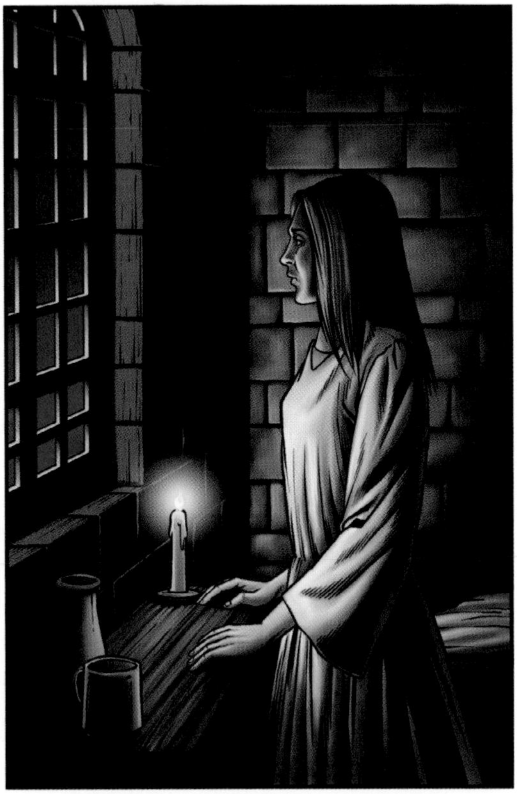

Báthory was imprisoned in her
own castle until her death.

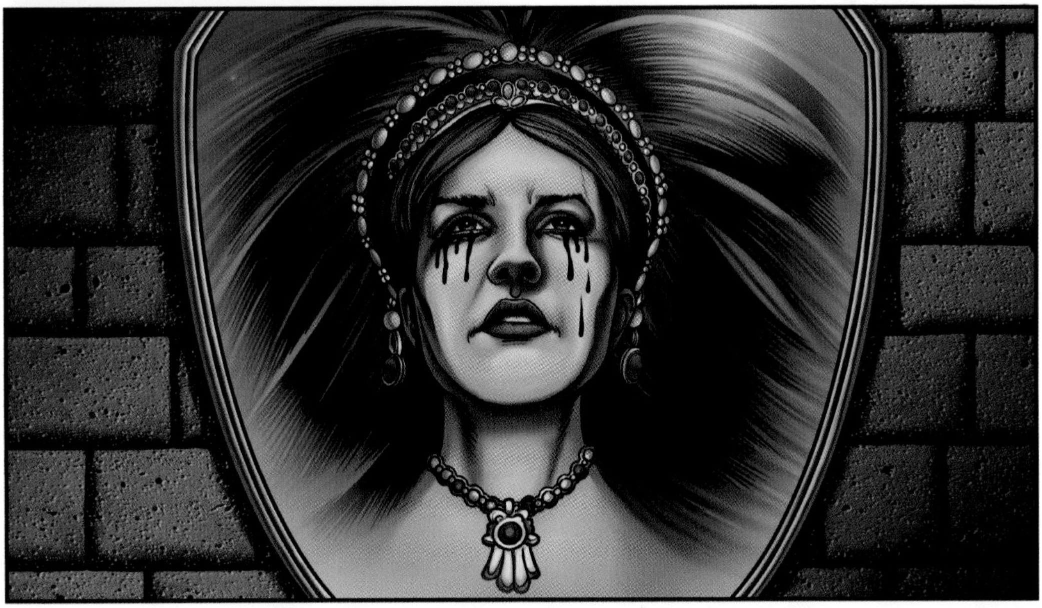

Was the Blood Countess the real Bloody Mary?

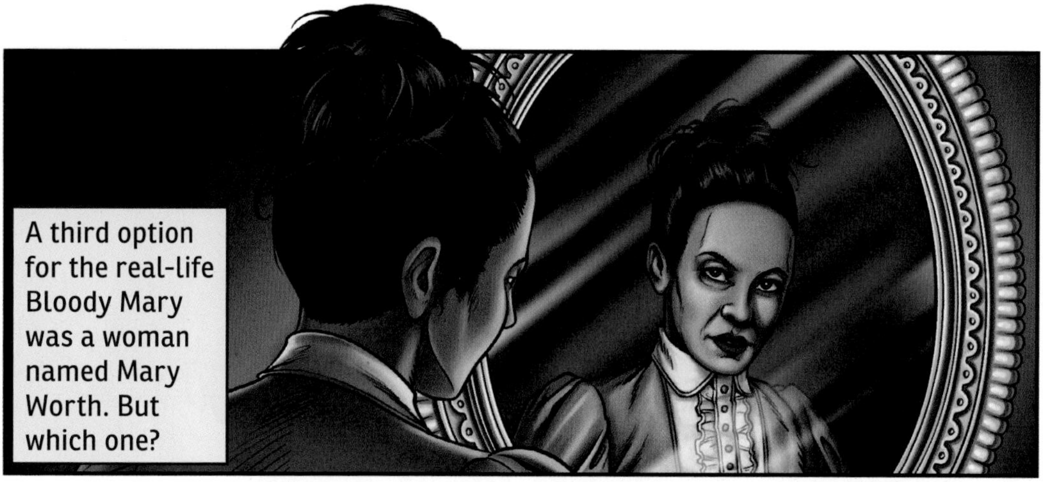
A third option for the real-life Bloody Mary was a woman named Mary Worth. But which one?

One Mary Worth lived in the 1600s. She was accused of witchcraft.

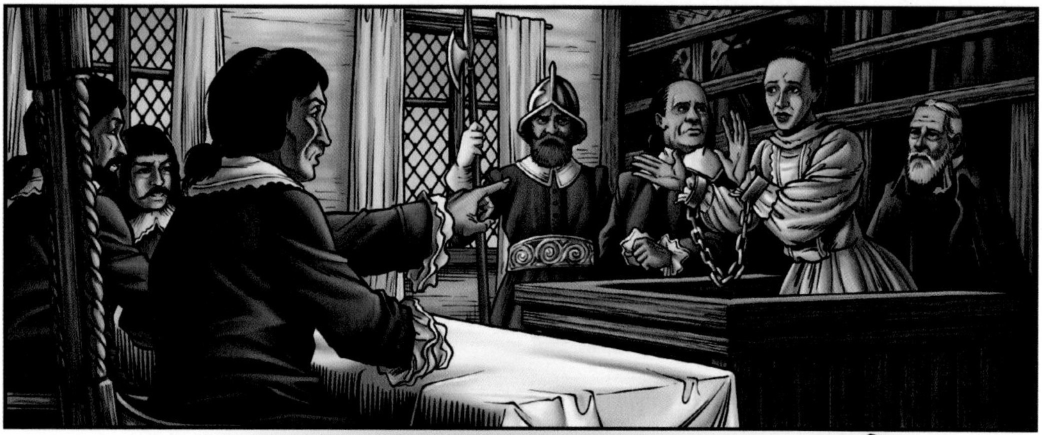

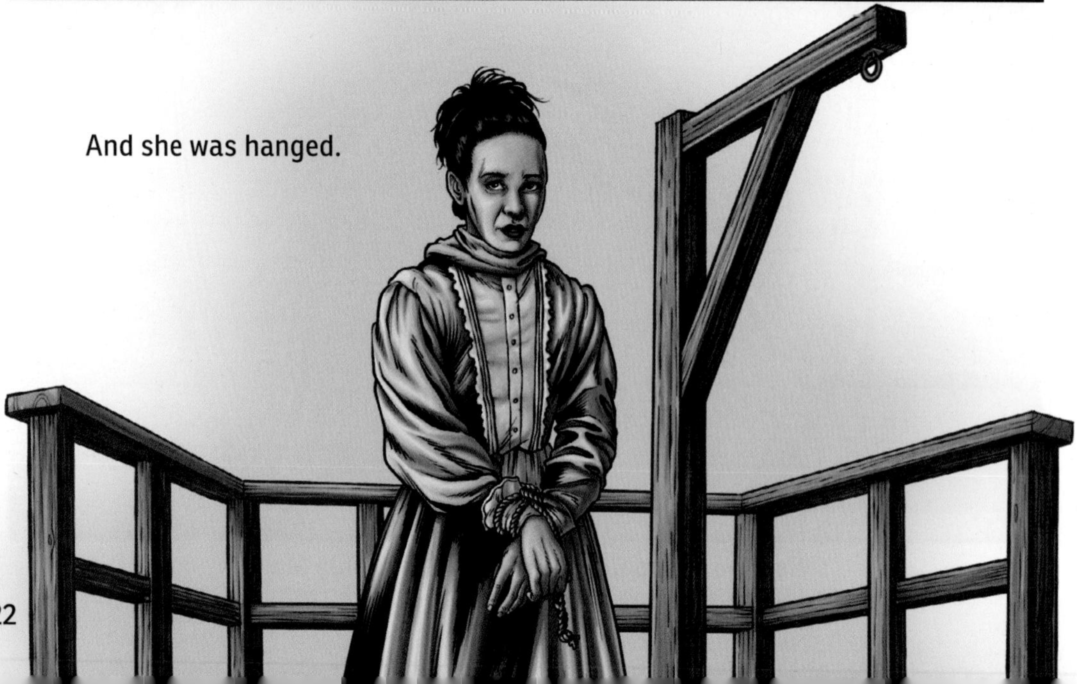
And she was hanged.

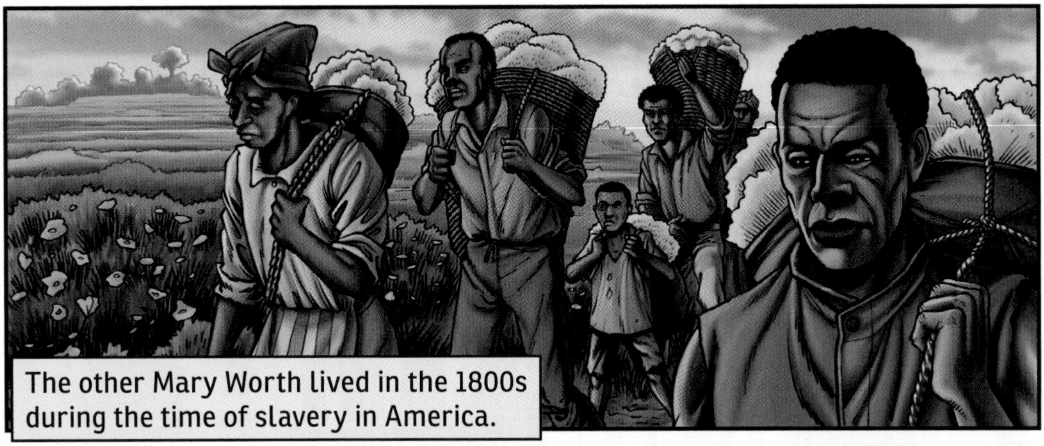
The other Mary Worth lived in the 1800s during the time of slavery in America.

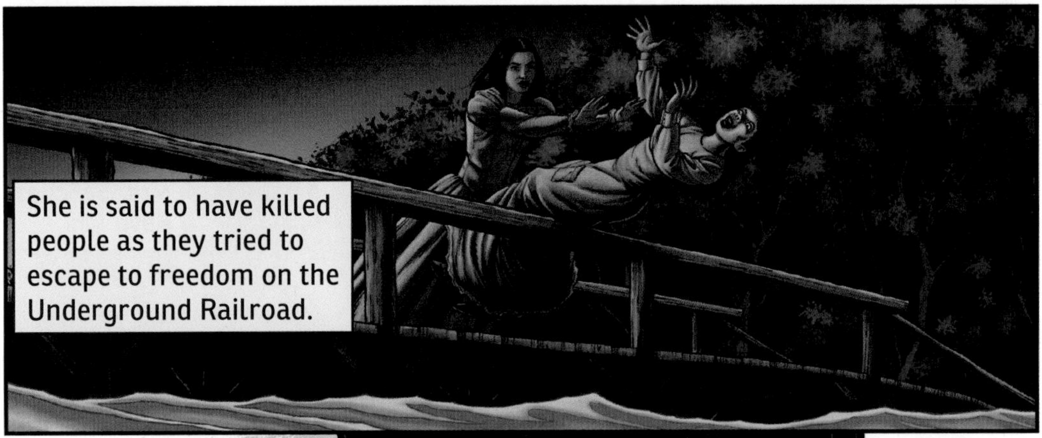
She is said to have killed people as they tried to escape to freedom on the Underground Railroad.

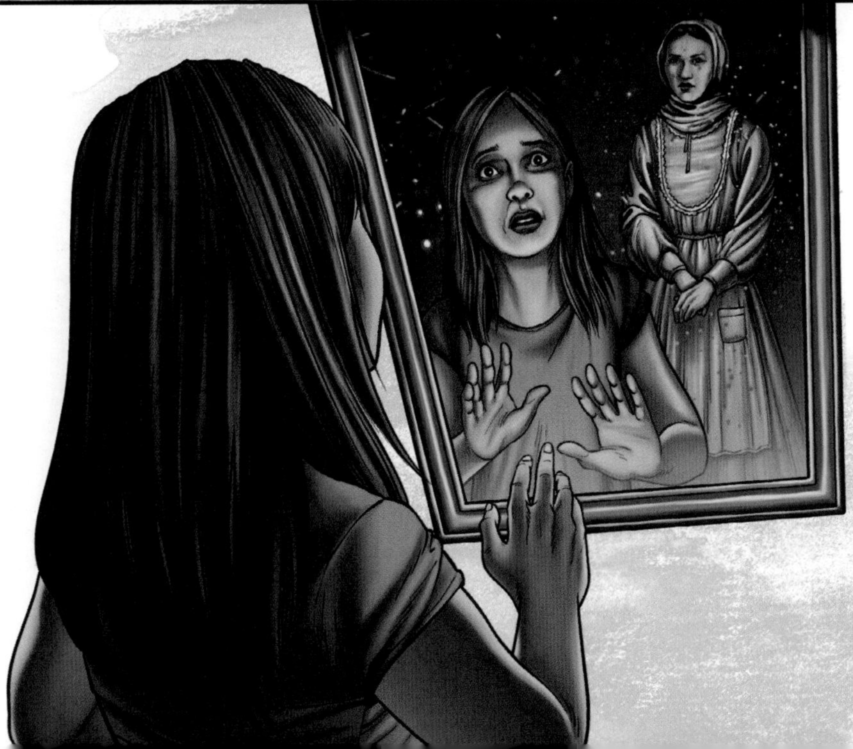

Could either of these Mary Worths be the inspiration for the real-life encounters with Bloody Mary that lie ahead?

CHAPTER 3
BLOODY MARY LIES IN WAIT

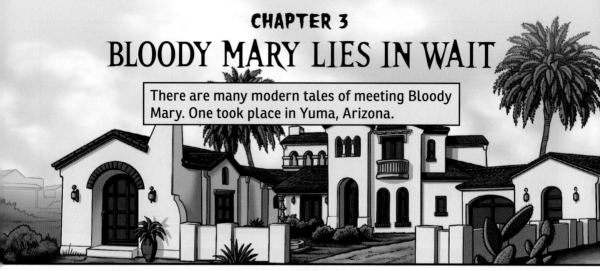

There are many modern tales of meeting Bloody Mary. One took place in Yuma, Arizona.

A girl named Cristina was visiting her friend.

I'm taking Maria shopping, Cristina. Can you watch the house while we're gone?

Sure thing, Mrs. Sanchez. Have fun!

This is boring. Gotta find something to do.

Maybe I'll play a game. All I need are some candles.

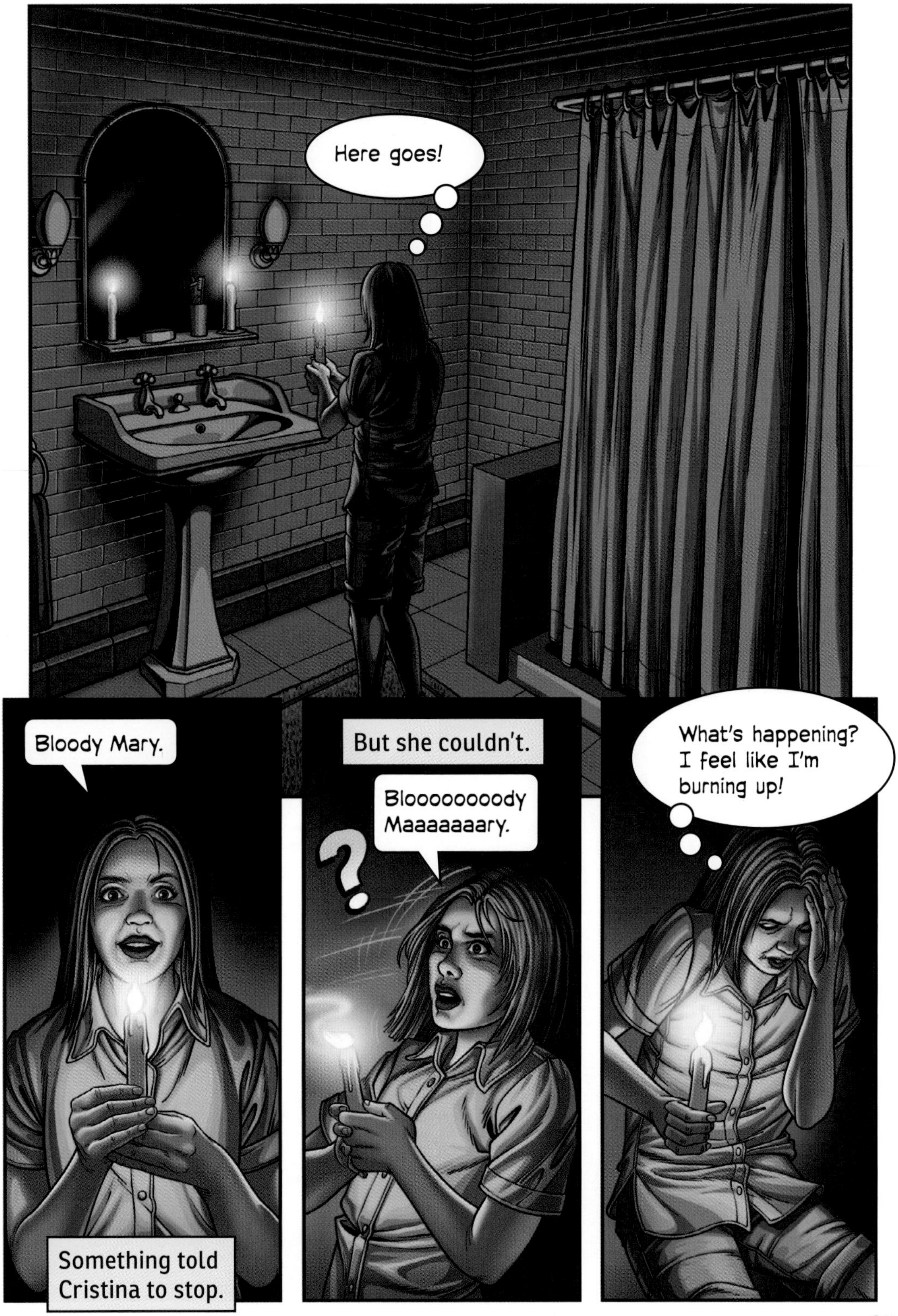
Here goes!
Bloody Mary.
Something told Cristina to stop.
But she couldn't.
Blooooooooody Maaaaaaary.
?
What's happening? I feel like I'm burning up!

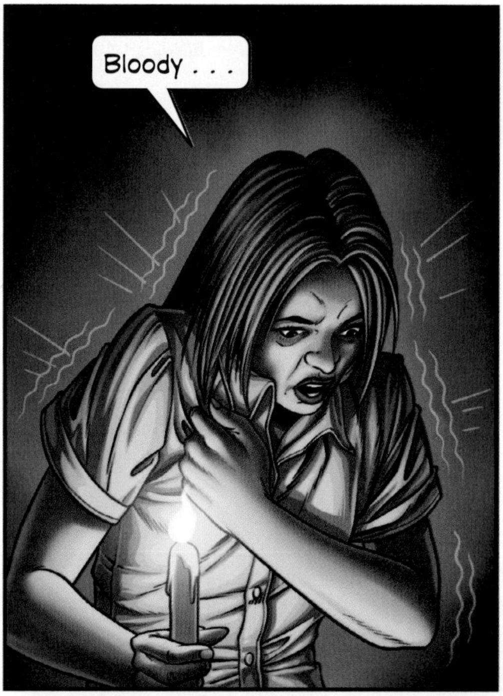
Bloody . . .

A sharp, cold wind suddenly blasted Cristina.

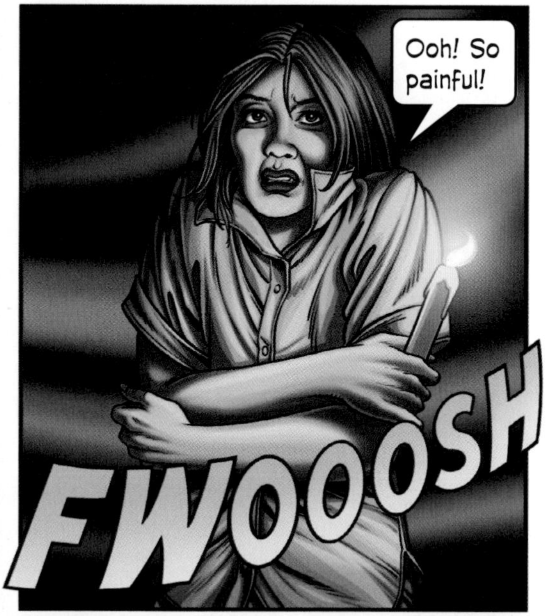
Ooh! So painful!
FWOOOSH

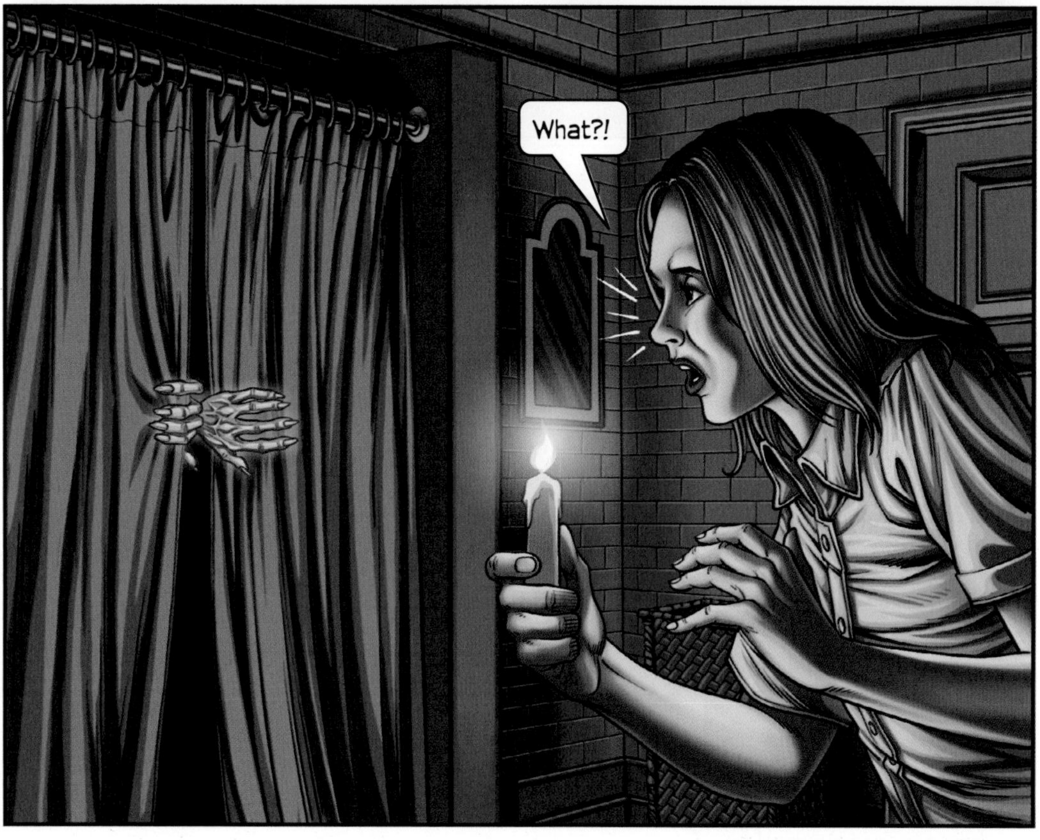
What?!

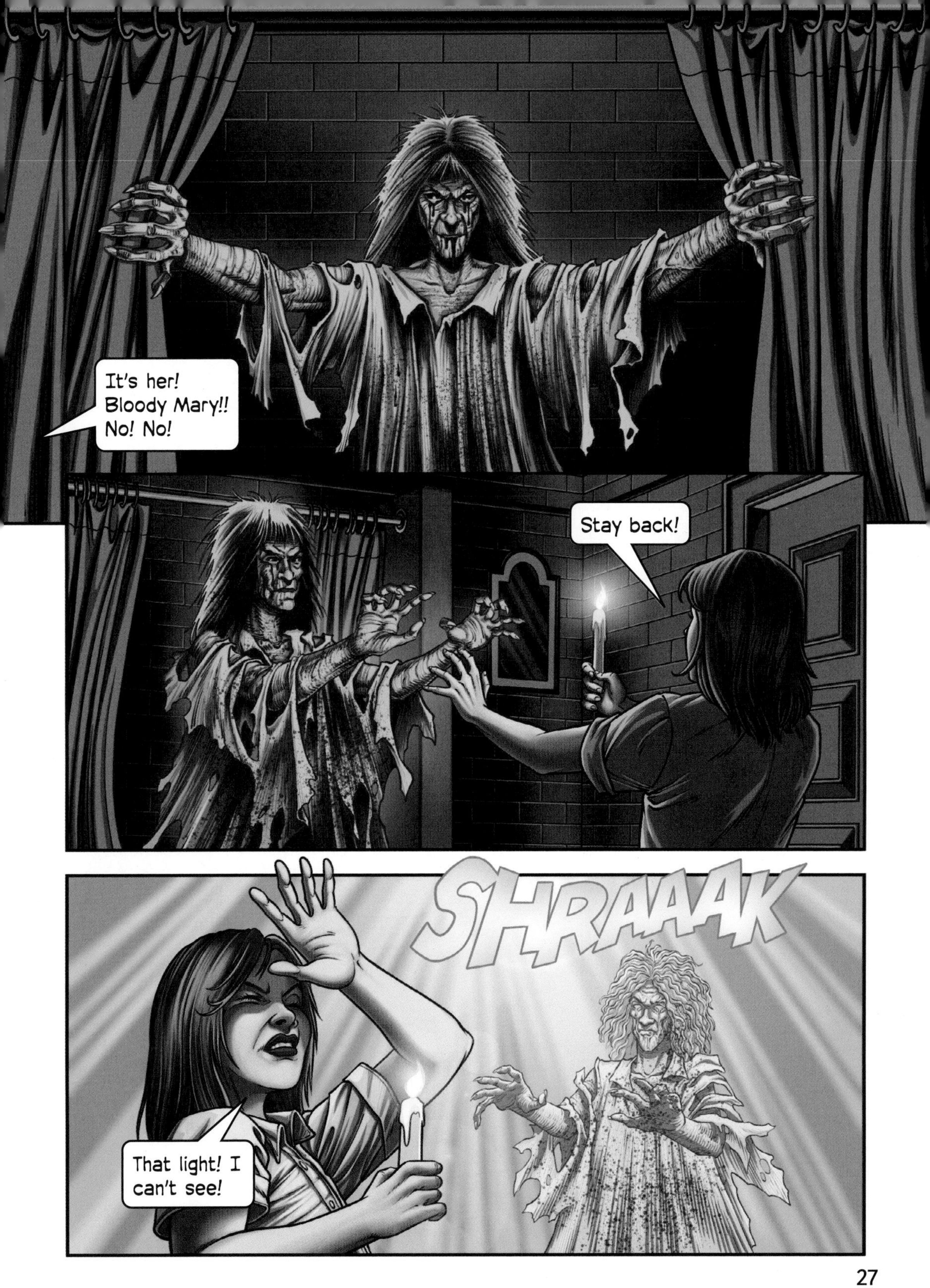
It's her! Bloody Mary!! No! No!
Stay back!
SHRAAAK
That light! I can't see!

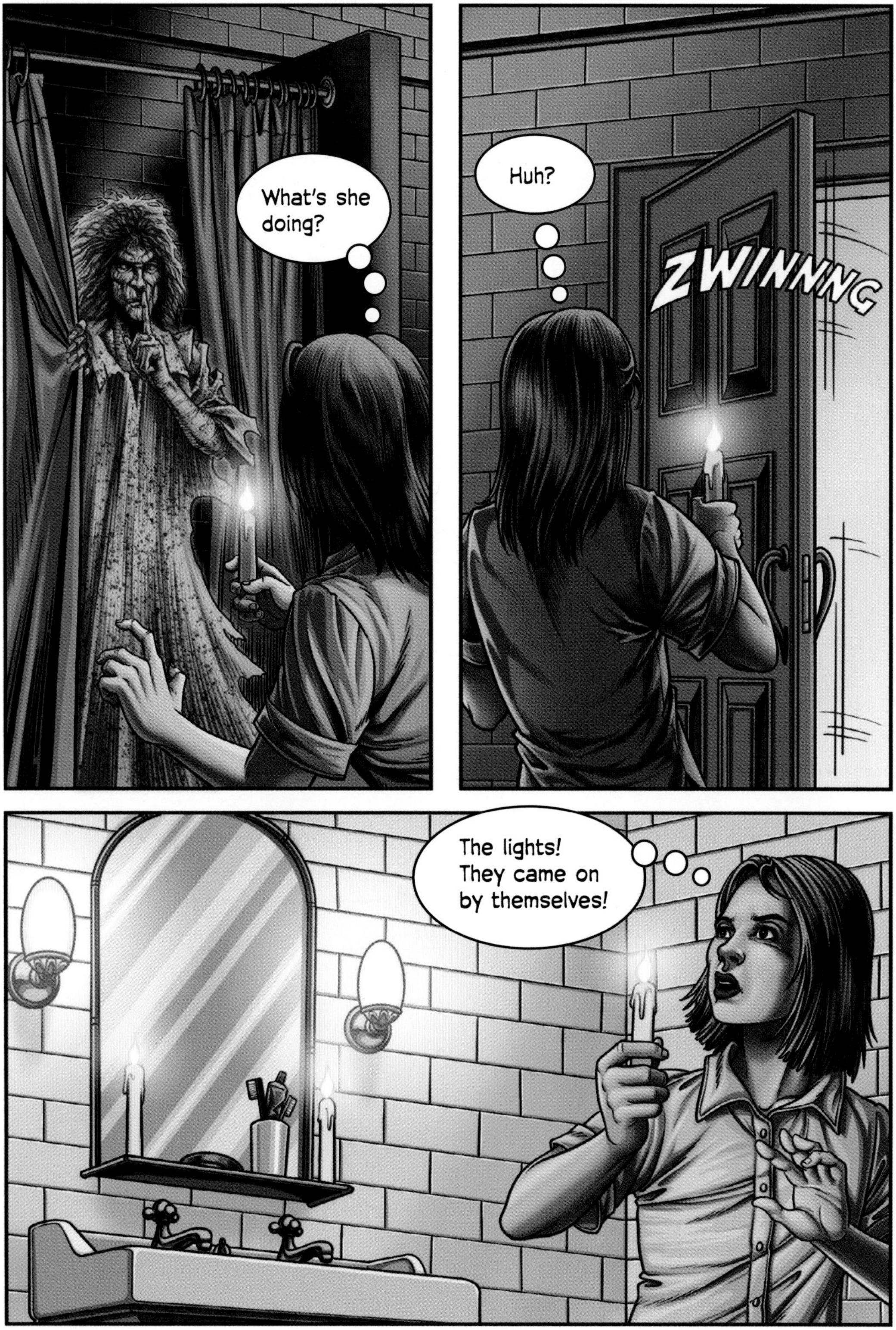
What's she doing?
Huh?
ZWINNNG
The lights! They came on by themselves!

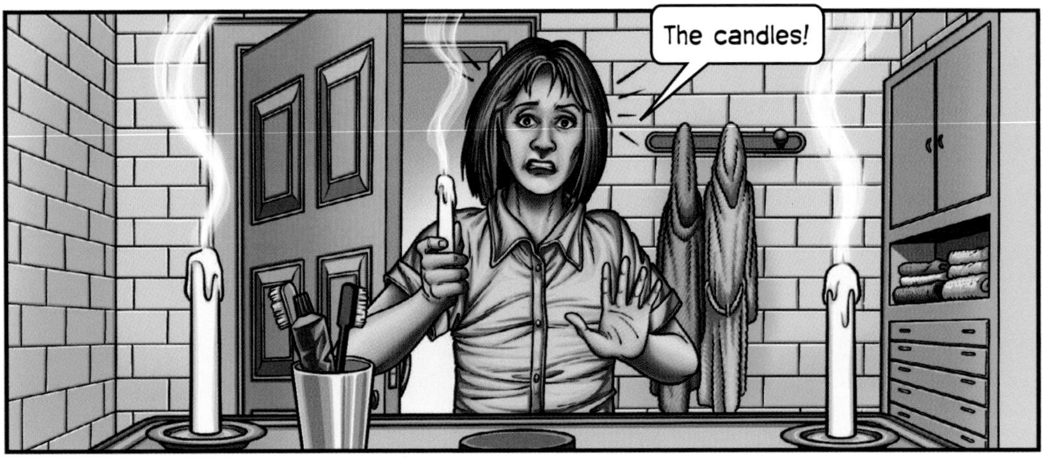
The candles!

Soon, Maria and her mother returned home.

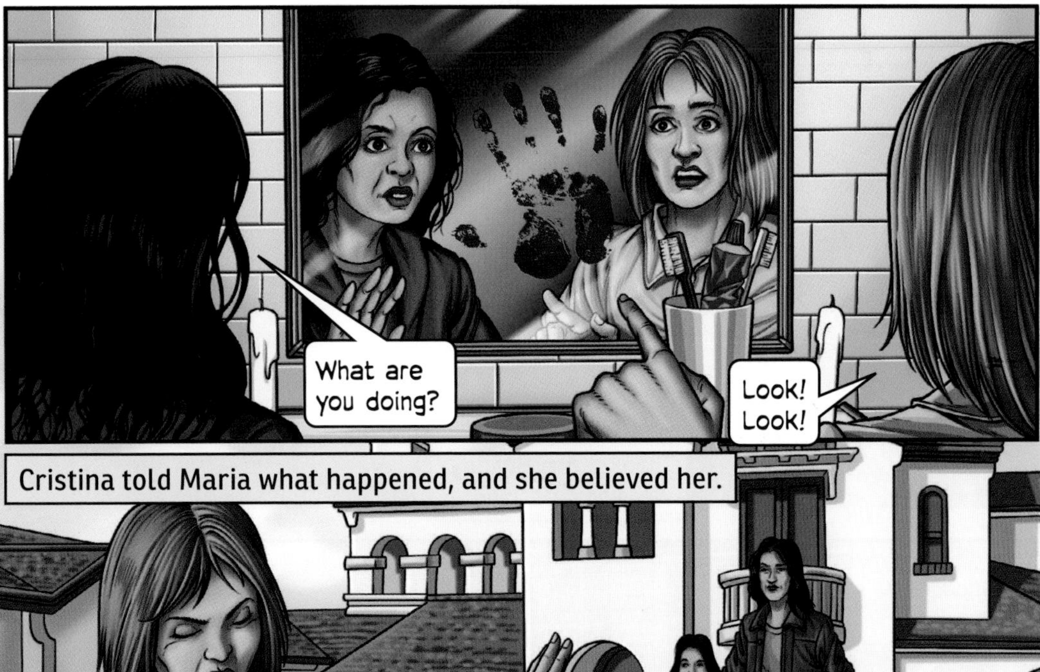
What are you doing?
Look! Look!

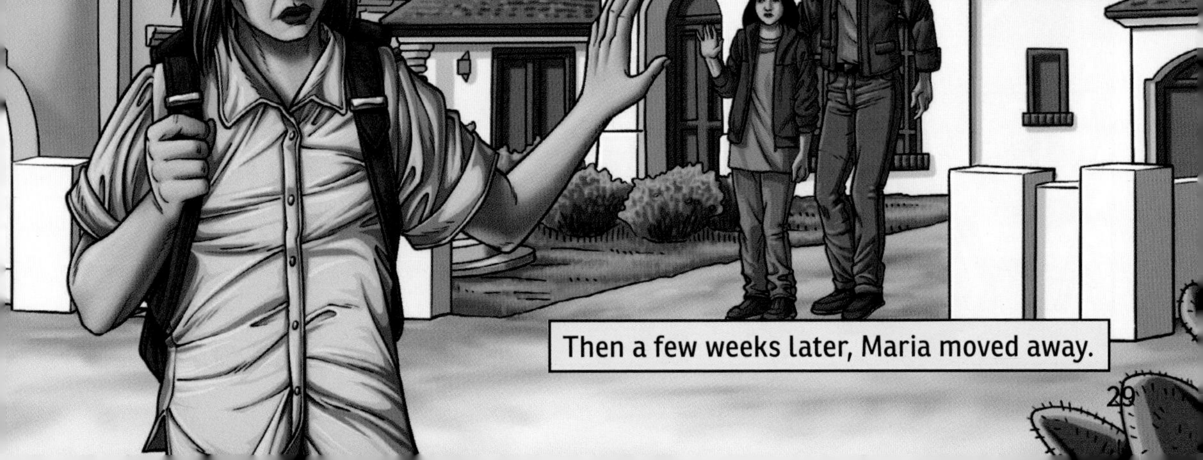
Cristina told Maria what happened, and she believed her.
Then a few weeks later, Maria moved away.

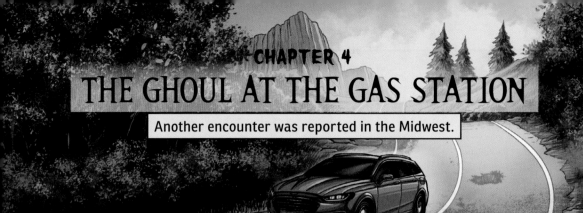

CHAPTER 4
THE GHOUL AT THE GAS STATION

Another encounter was reported in the Midwest.

Lauren and her friend Kate took a weekend vacation with Lauren's parents.

Time for a pit stop! You can hit the restrooms while we gas up the car, girls.

Thanks, Mr. Holiday. We won't be long.

Wanna have some fun?

I'm game. What's up?

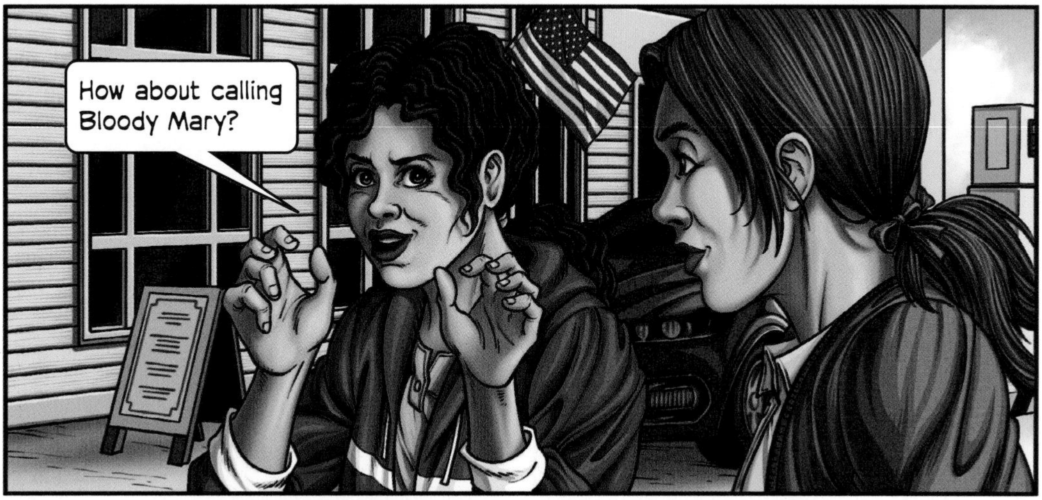
How about calling Bloody Mary?

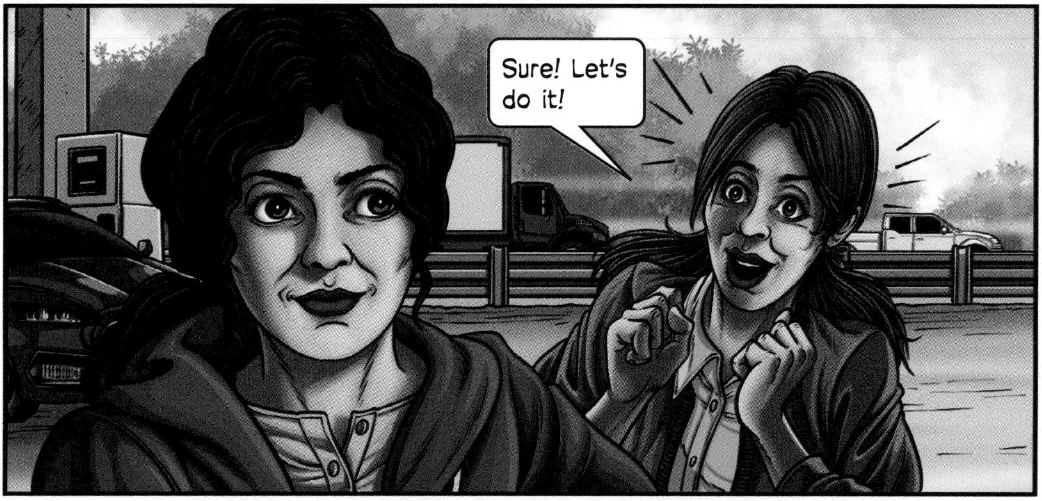
Sure! Let's do it!

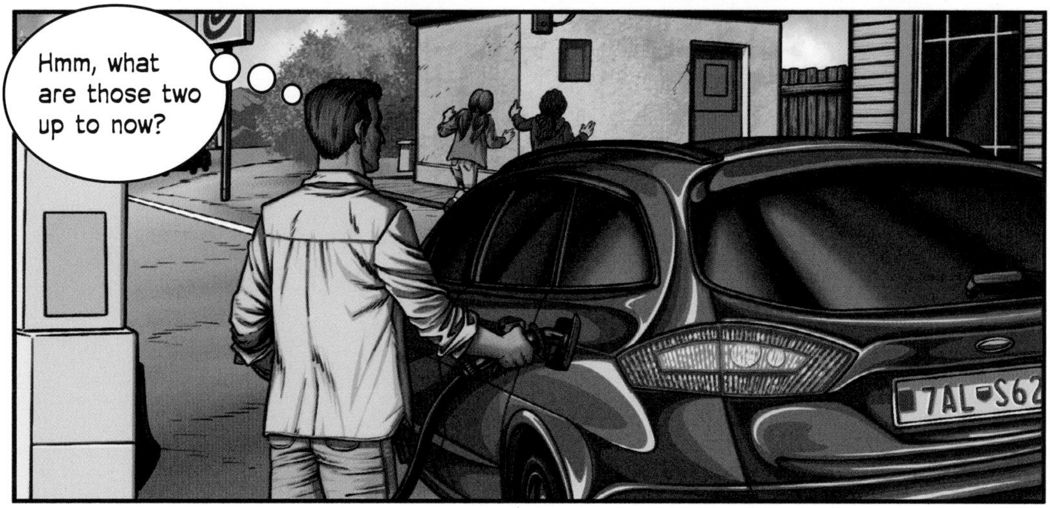
Hmm, what are those two up to now?

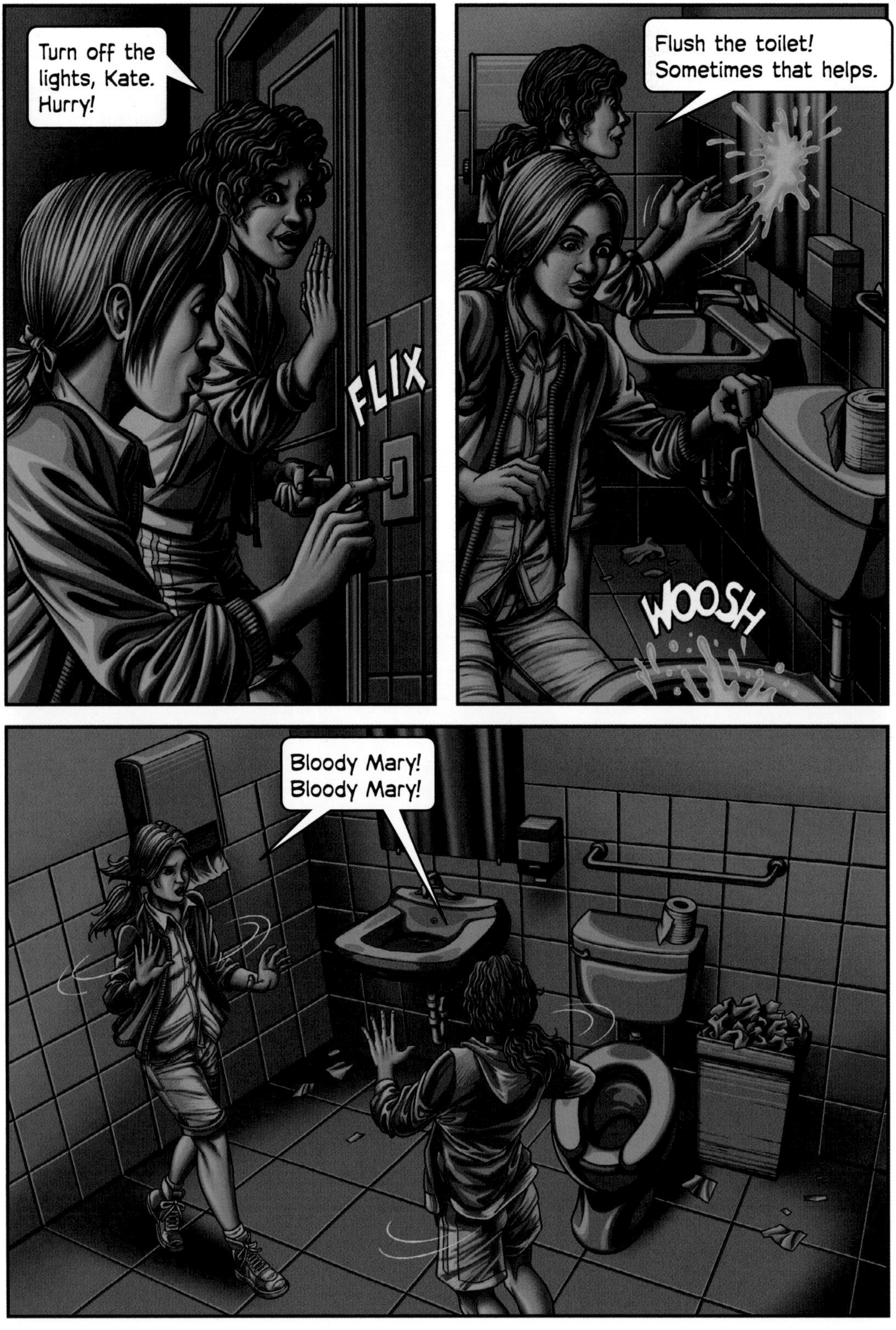
Turn off the lights, Kate. Hurry!
FLIX
Flush the toilet! Sometimes that helps.
WOOSH
Bloody Mary! Bloody Mary!

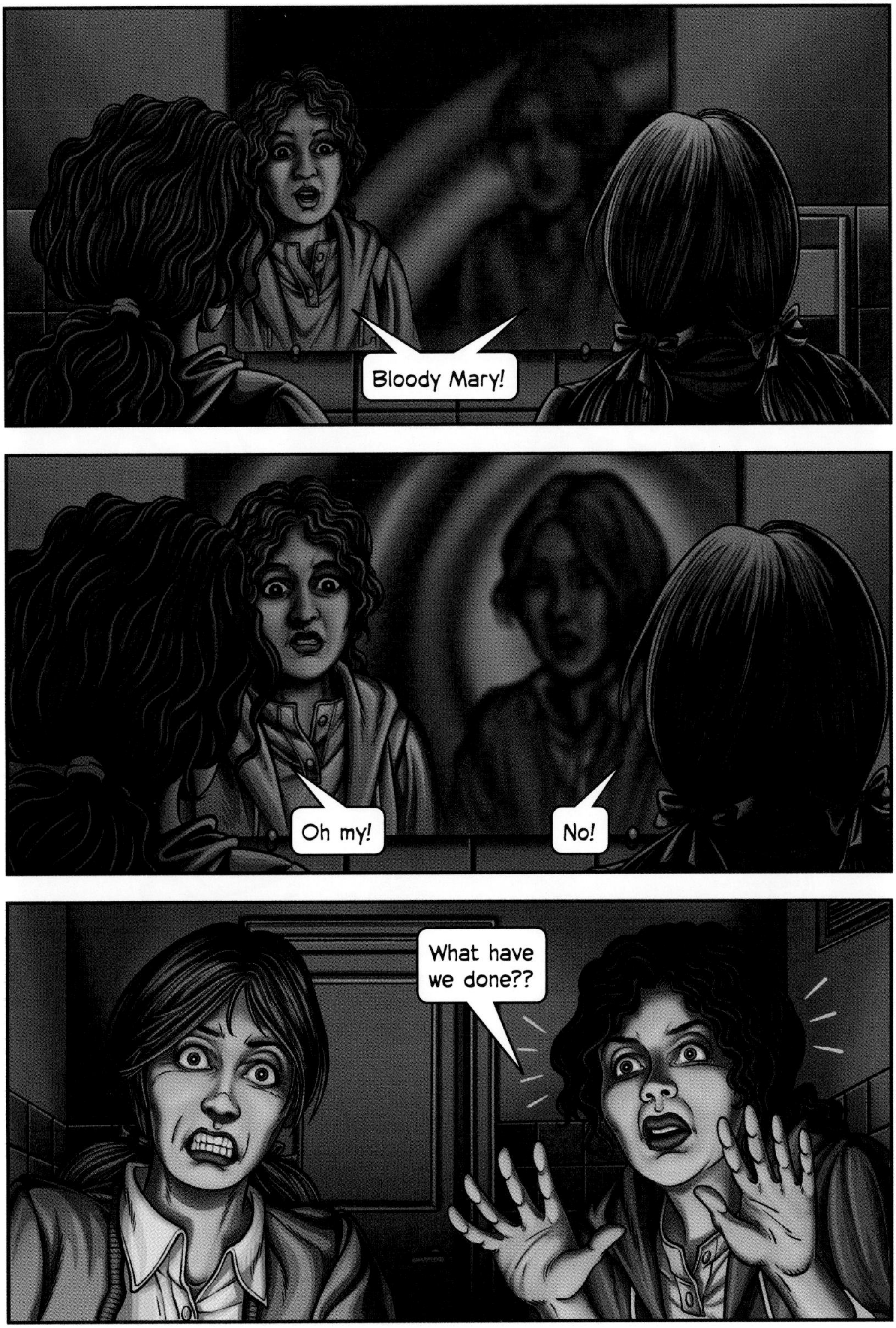
Bloody Mary!
Oh my!
No!
What have we done??

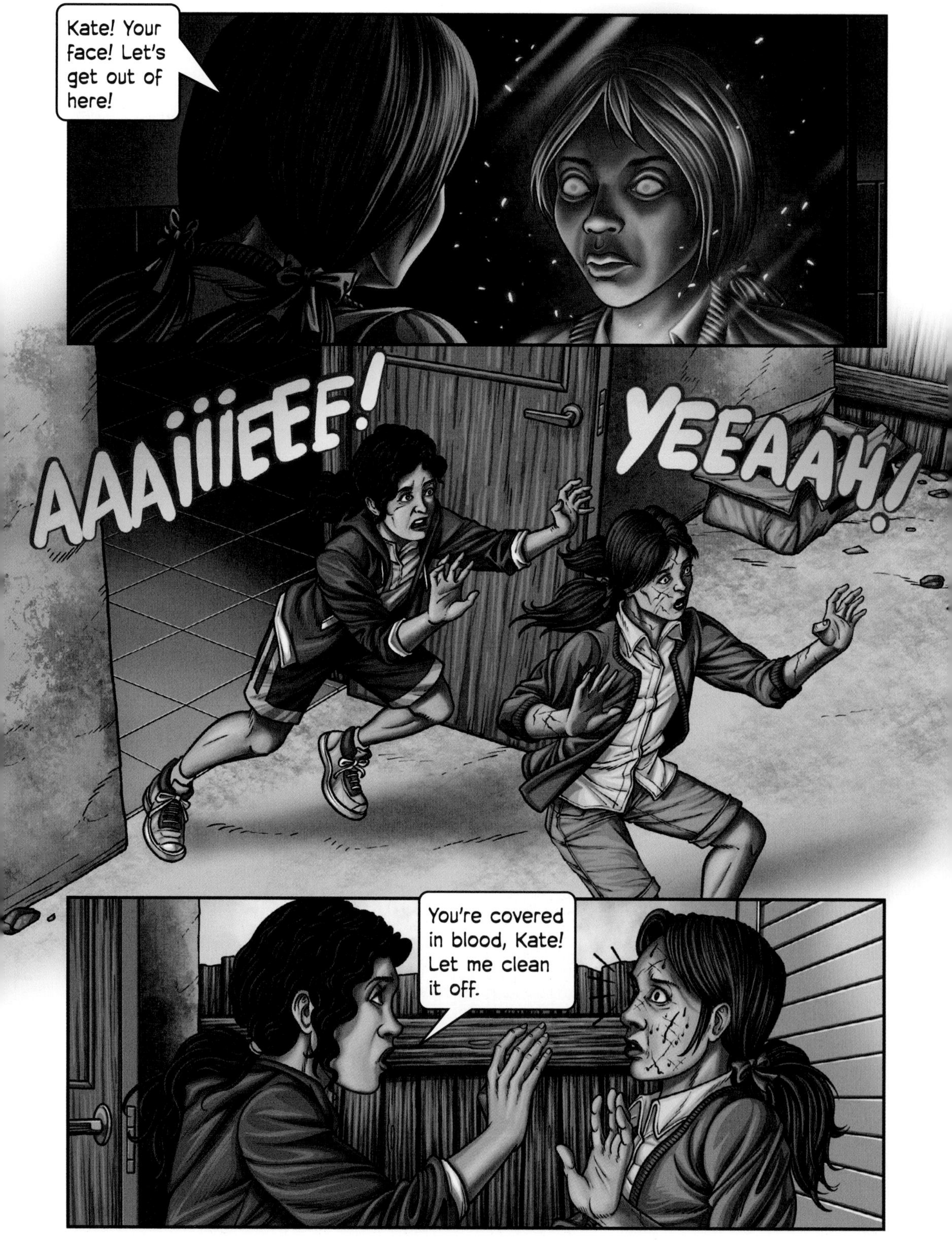
Kate! Your face! Let's get out of here!
AAAiiiiEEEE!
YEEAAH!
You're covered in blood, Kate! Let me clean it off.

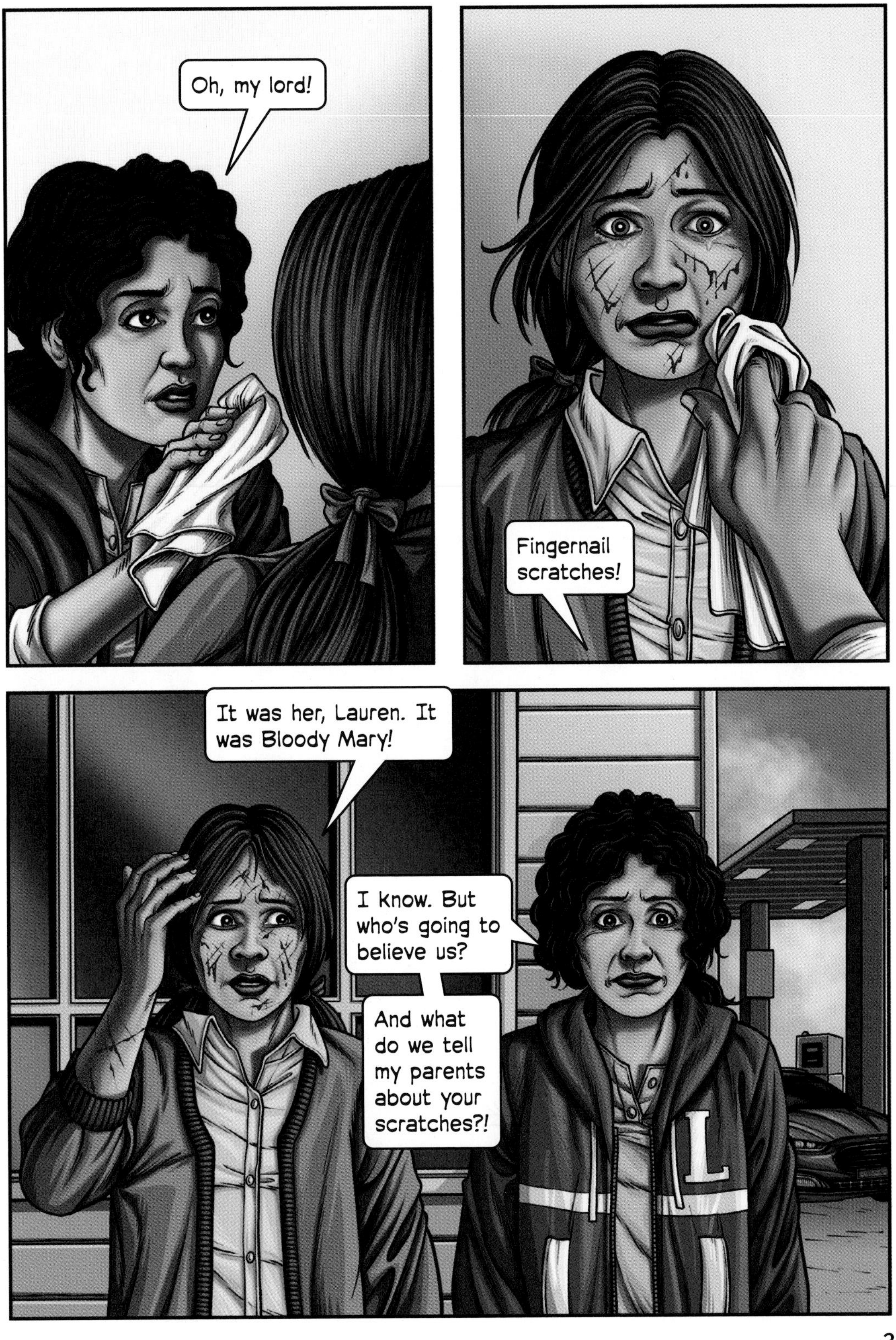
Oh, my lord!
Fingernail scratches!
It was her, Lauren. It was Bloody Mary!
I know. But who's going to believe us?
And what do we tell my parents about your scratches?!

CHAPTER 5
THE SINISTER SLUMBER PARTY

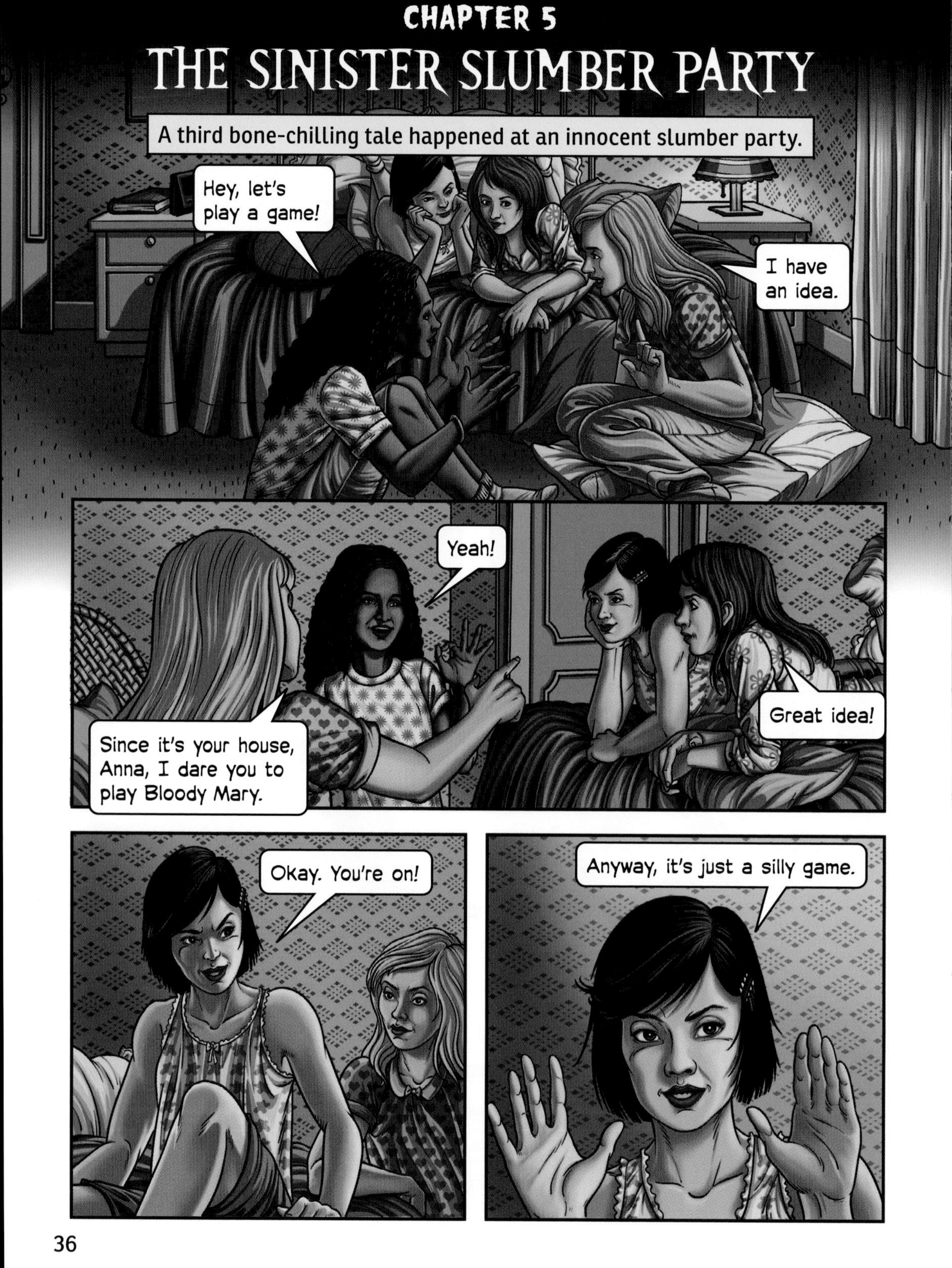

A third bone-chilling tale happened at an innocent slumber party.
Hey, let's play a game!
I have an idea.
Since it's your house, Anna, I dare you to play Bloody Mary.
Yeah!
Great idea!
Okay. You're on!
Anyway, it's just a silly game.

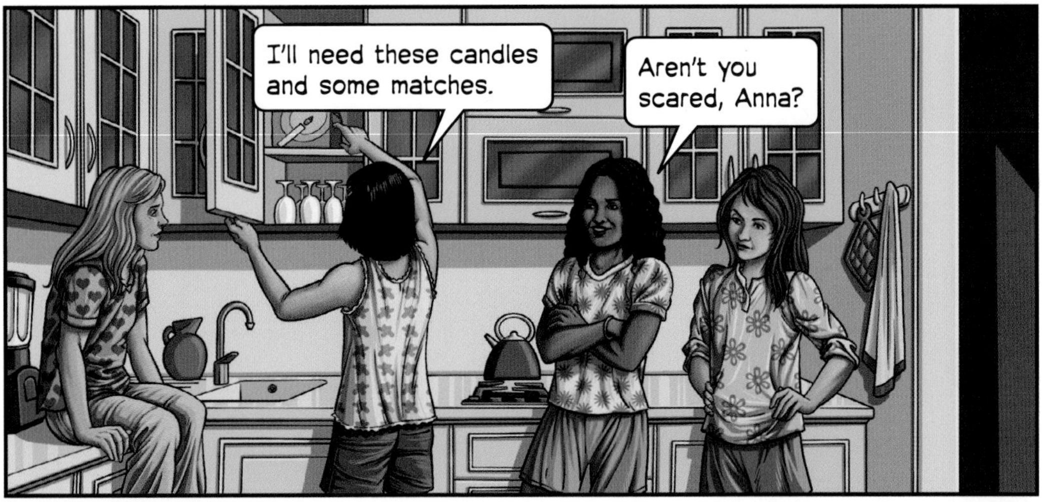
I'll need these candles and some matches.
Aren't you scared, Anna?

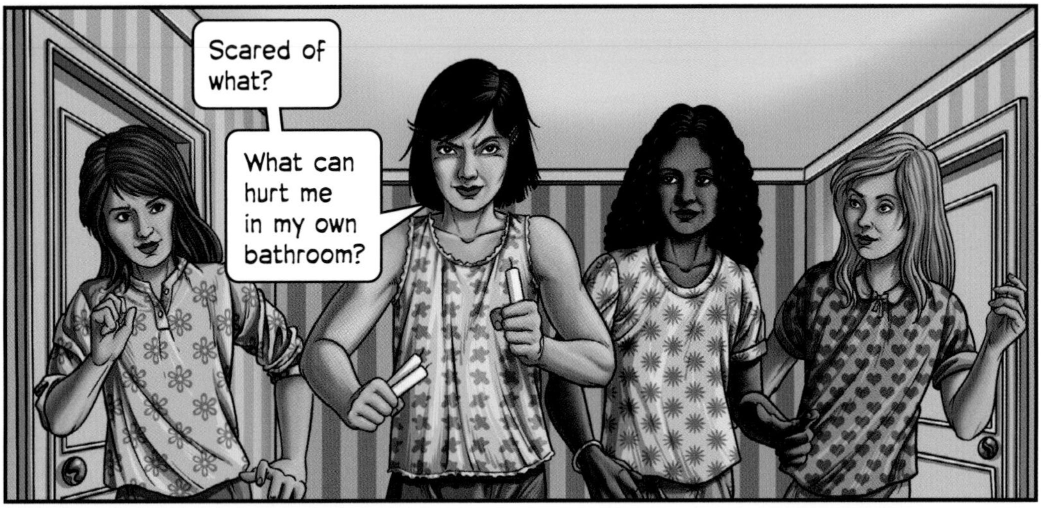
Scared of what?
What can hurt me in my own bathroom?

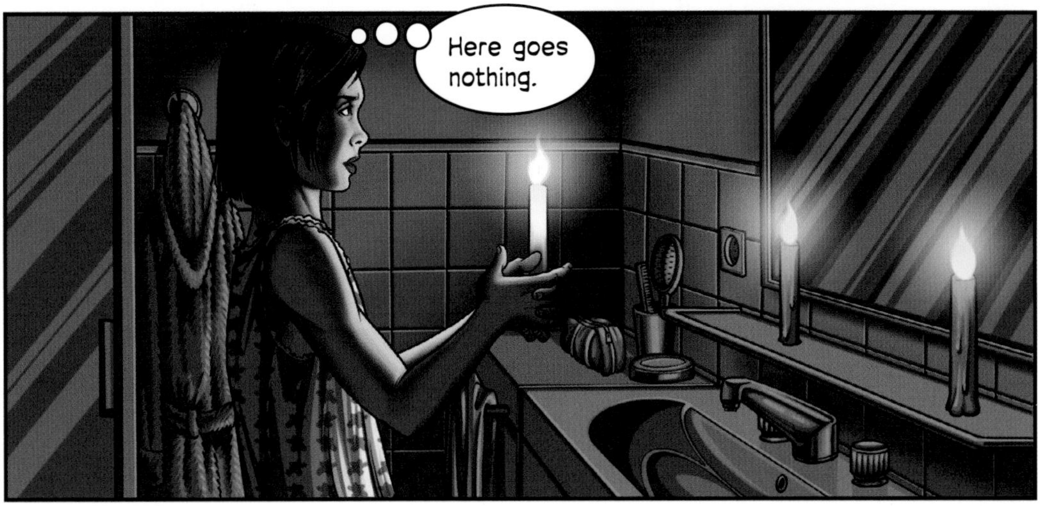
Here goes nothing.

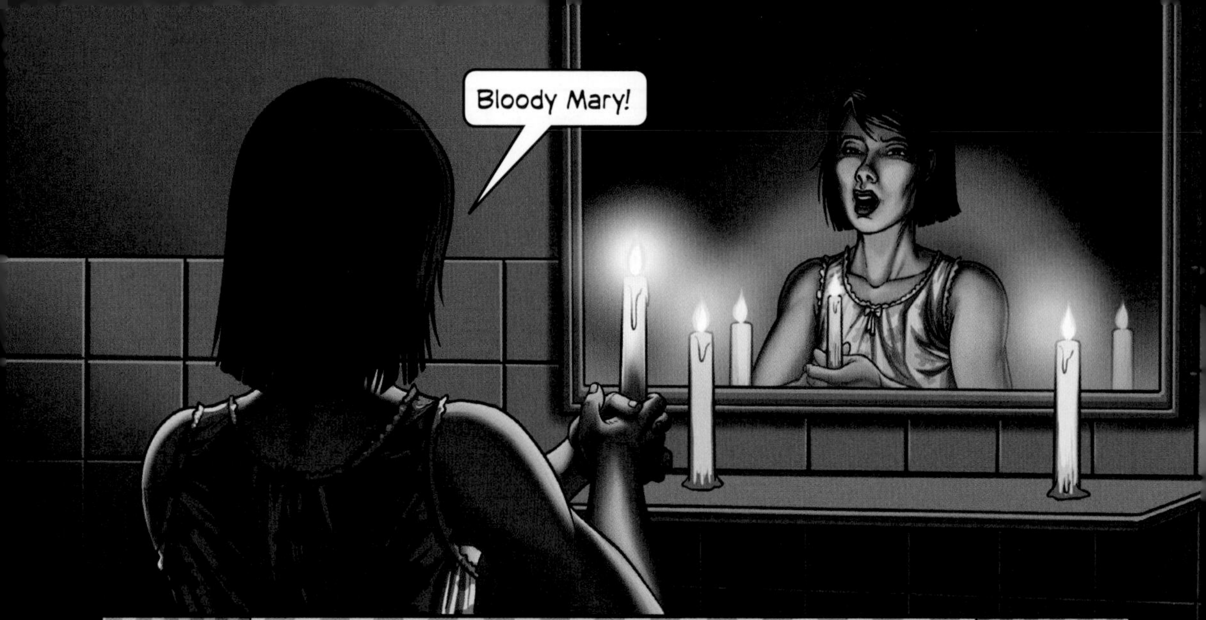
Bloody Mary!

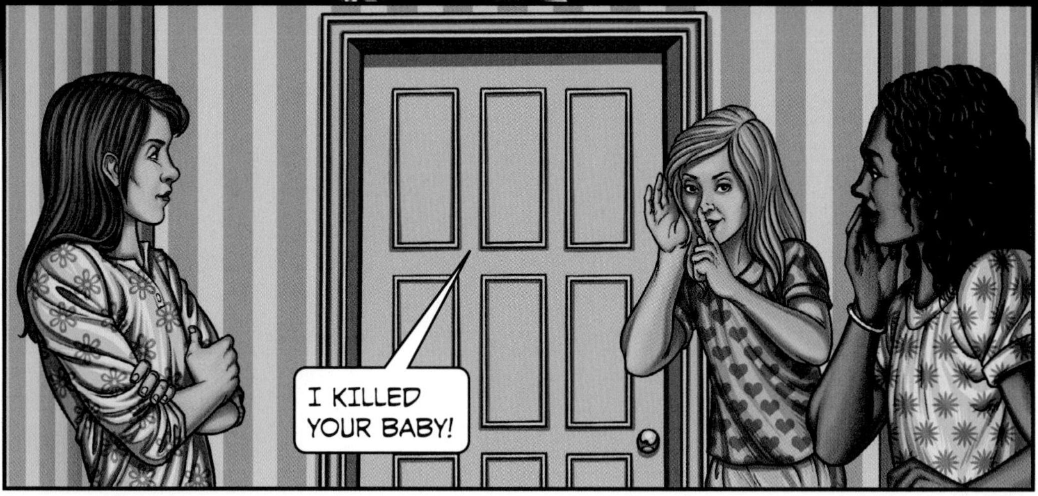
I KILLED
YOUR BABY!

Fifteen minutes passed in silence. And then . . .

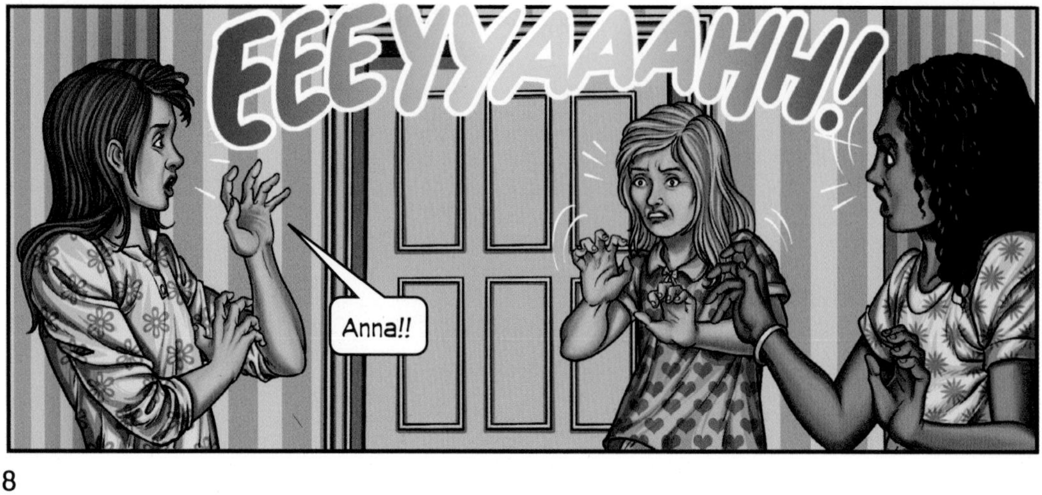
EEEYYAAAAHH!
Anna!!

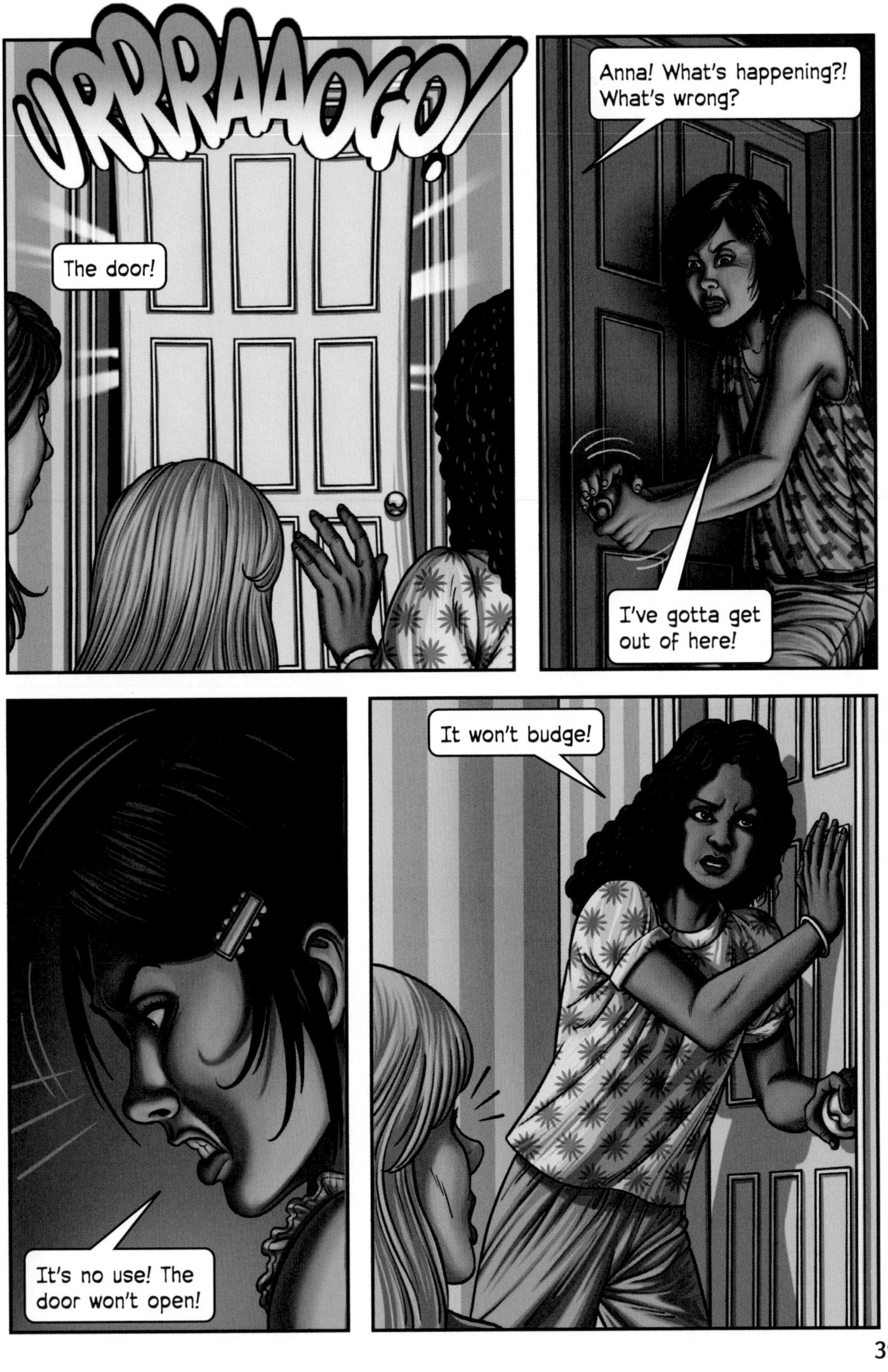
URRRAAOGO!
The door!
Anna! What's happening?! What's wrong?
I've gotta get out of here!
It's no use! The door won't open!
It won't budge!

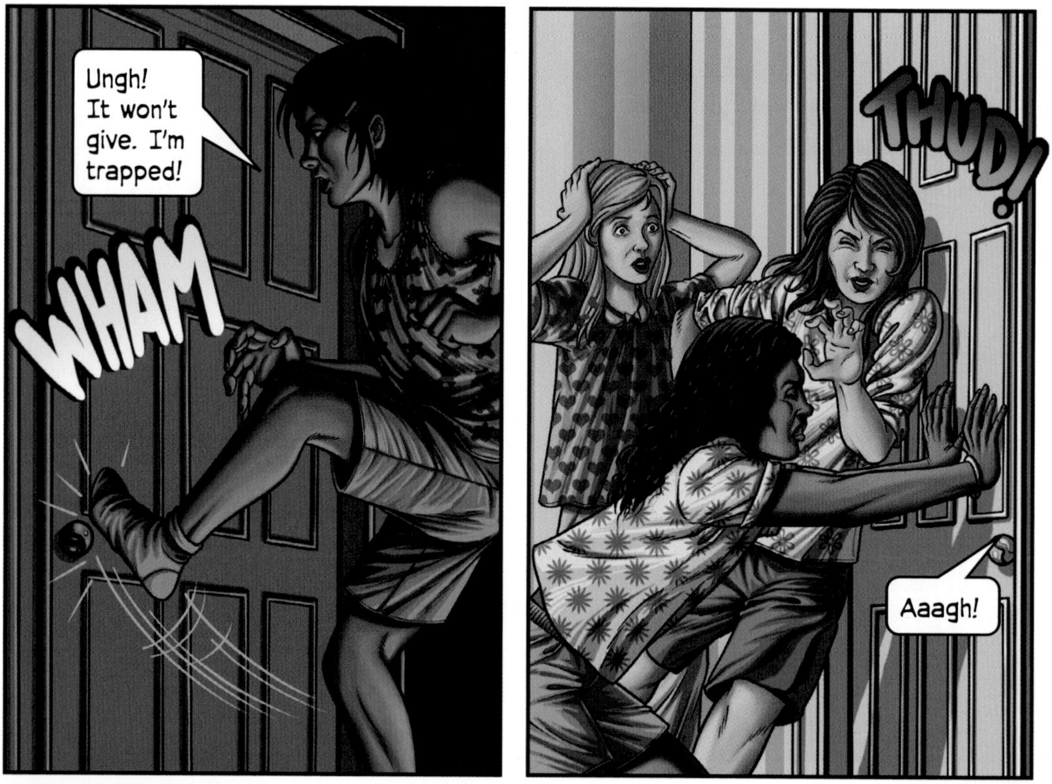
Ungh! It won't give. I'm trapped!
WHAM
THUD!
Aaagh!

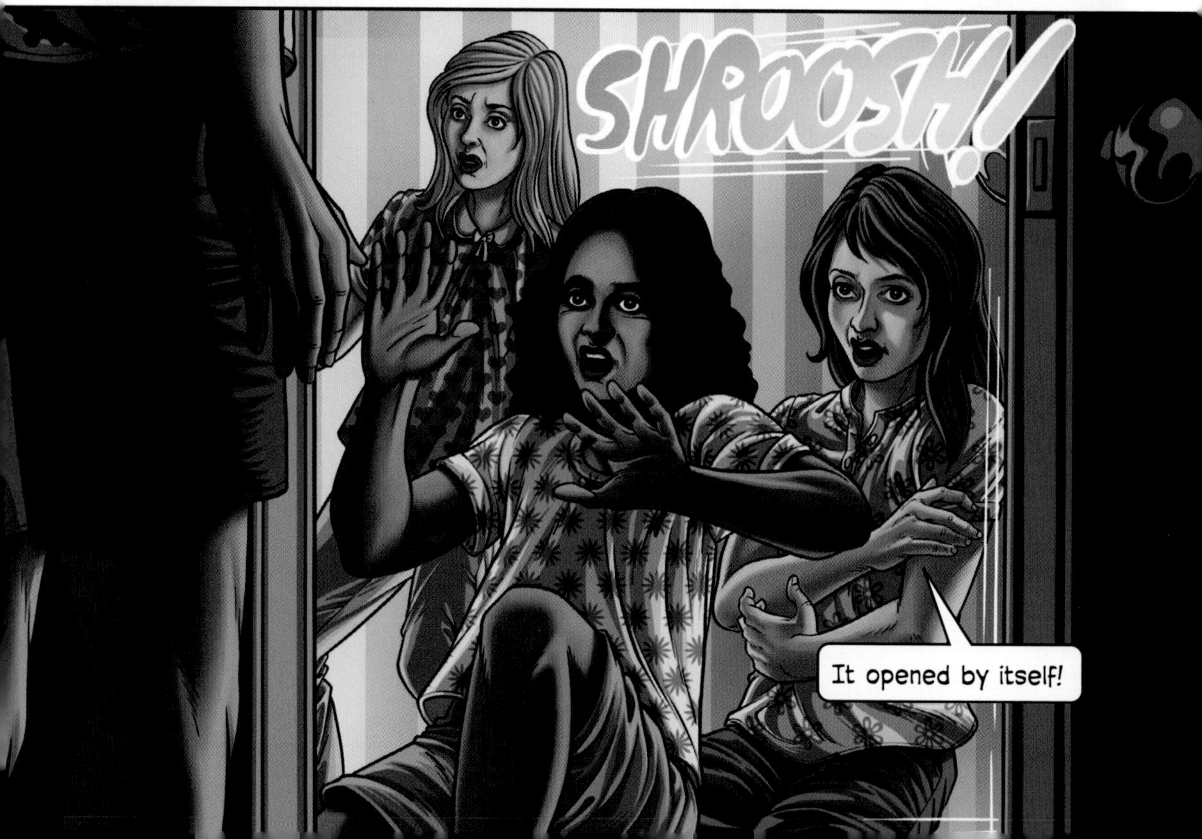
SHROOSH!
It opened by itself!

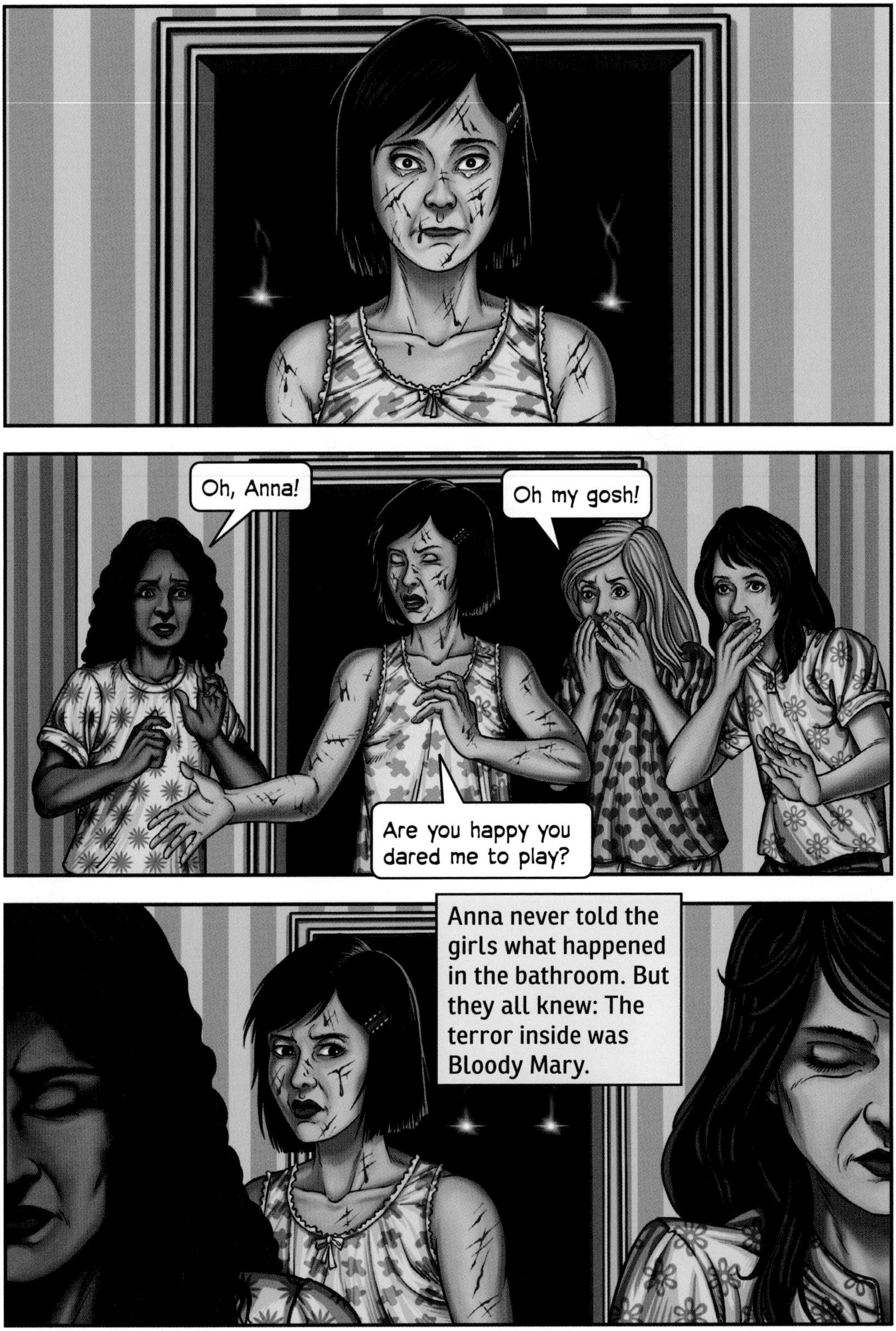
Oh, Anna!
Oh my gosh!
Are you happy you dared me to play?
Anna never told the girls what happened in the bathroom. But they all knew: The terror inside was Bloody Mary.

EPILOGUE
THE LURE OF BLOODY MARY

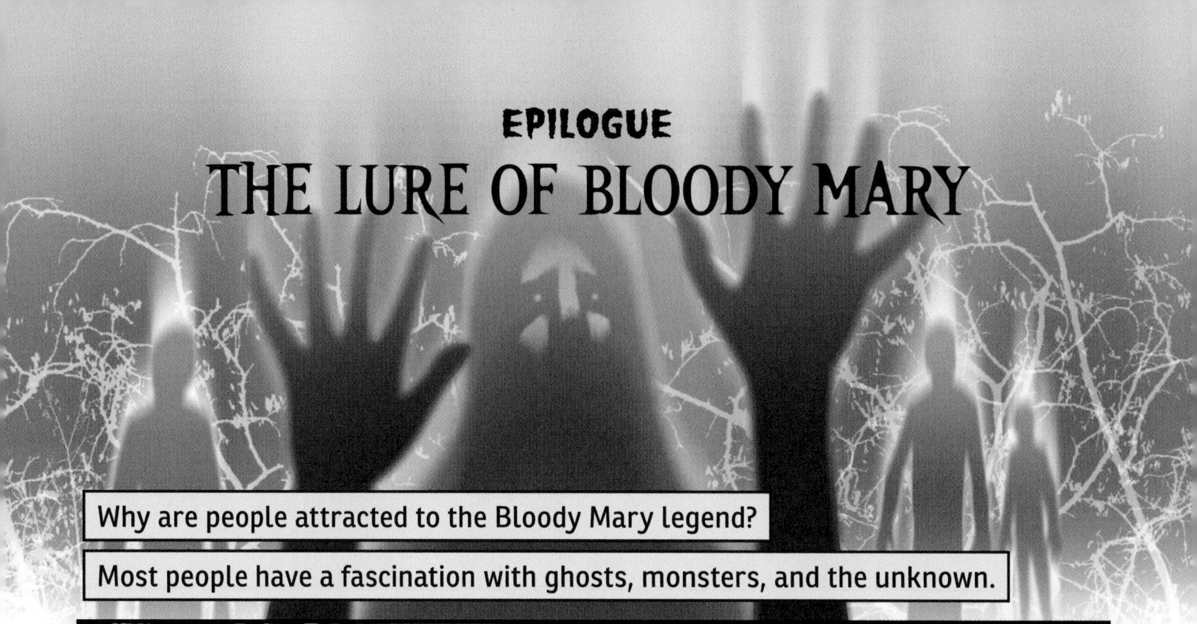
Why are people attracted to the Bloody Mary legend?
Most people have a fascination with ghosts, monsters, and the unknown.

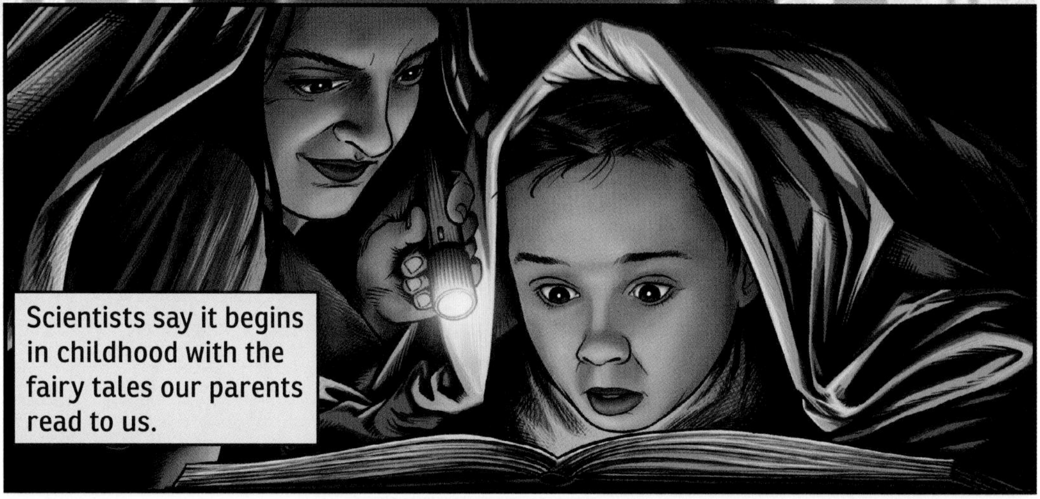
Scientists say it begins in childhood with the fairy tales our parents read to us.

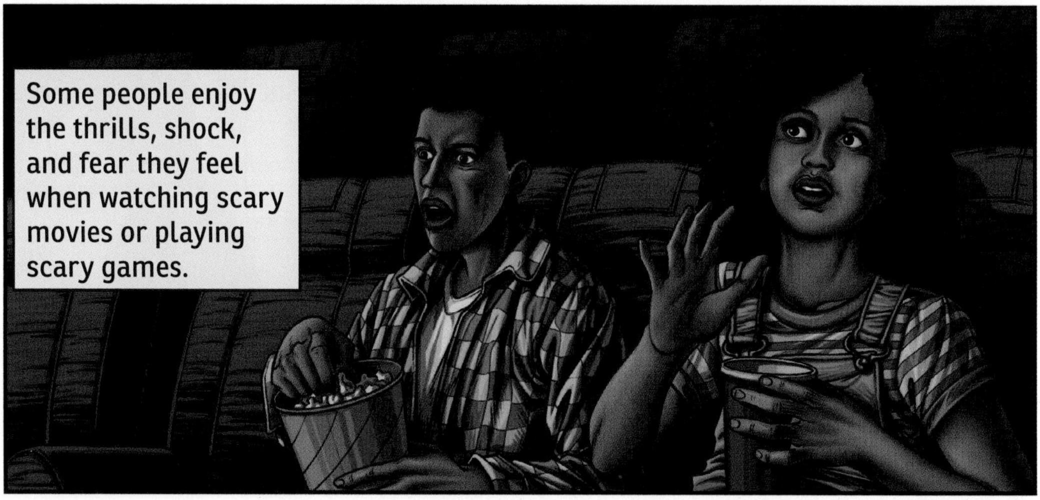
Some people enjoy the thrills, shock, and fear they feel when watching scary movies or playing scary games.

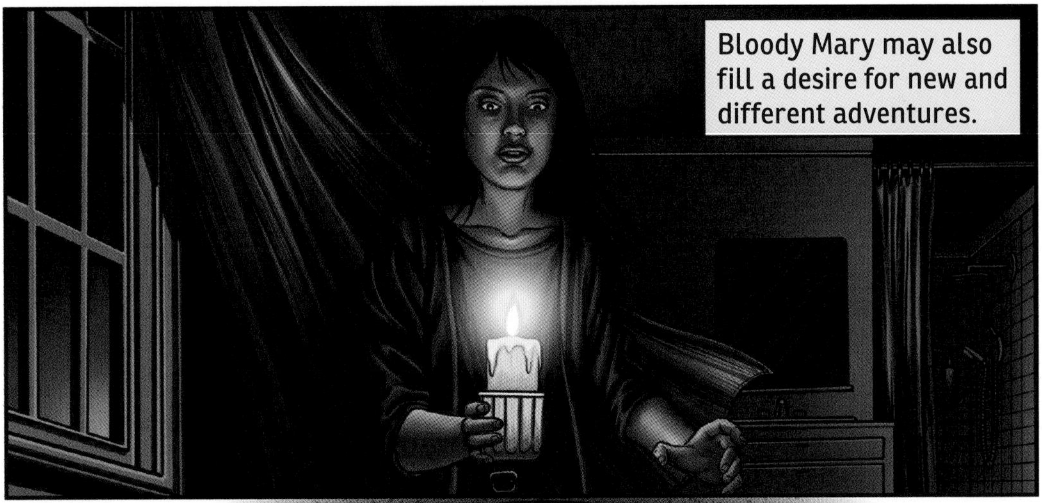
Bloody Mary may also fill a desire for new and different adventures.

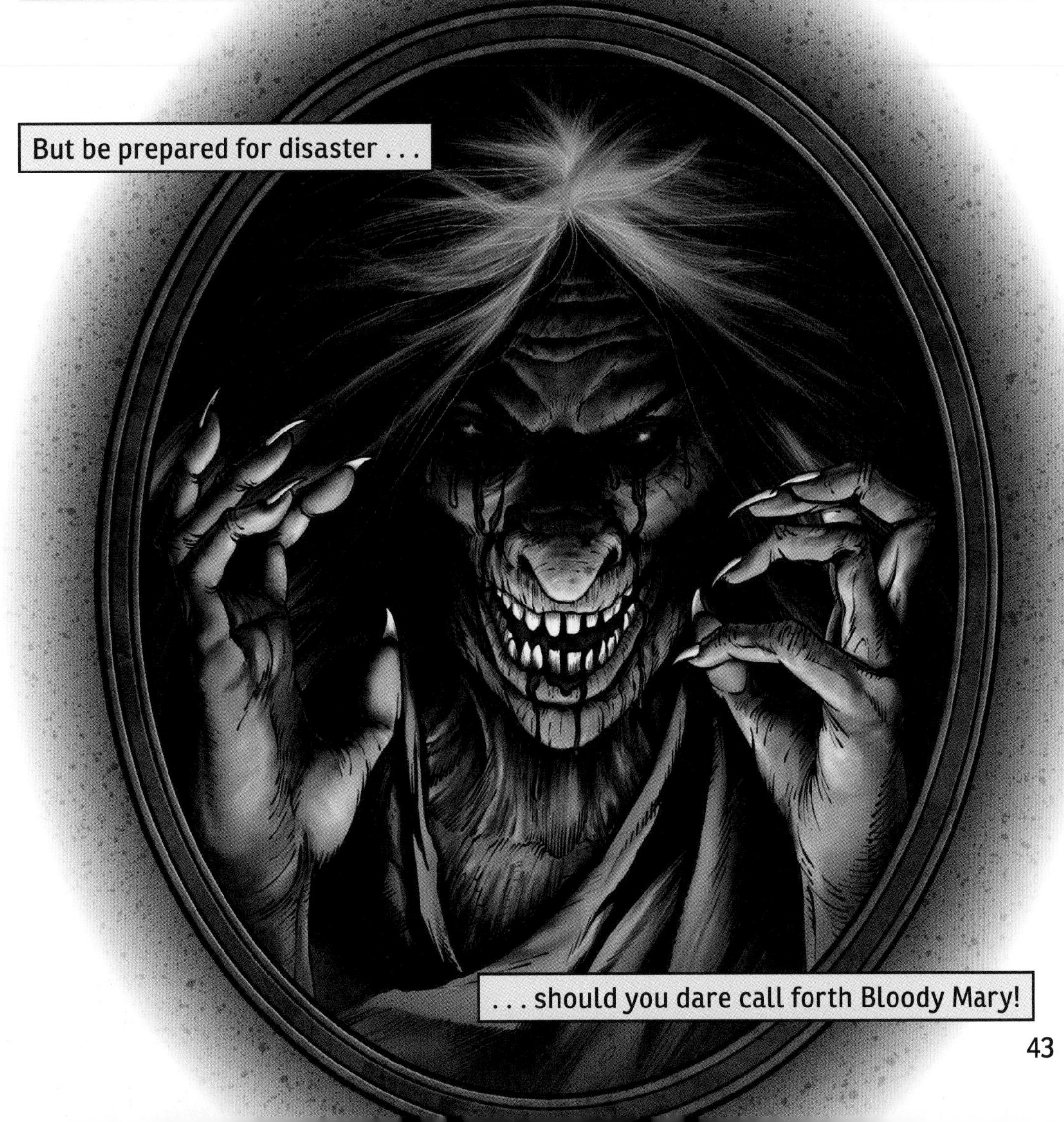
But be prepared for disaster . . .
. . . should you dare call forth Bloody Mary!

MORE ABOUT
BLOODY MARY

● Can we really see ghosts like Bloody Mary in mirrors? Science says we can. In 1804, a Swiss doctor proved that staring into a mirror can warp our surroundings into something weird and scary.

● In 2010, an Italian doctor found that staring at yourself in a mirror in a dimly lit room can cause you to see strange faces. What you're seeing are not actually ghosts. Your brain is just making something normal seem to be warped and frightening.

● Bloody Mary has been the subject of movies, books, and TV shows. She has even appeared in a video game.

● A famous Greek thinker encouraged people to look at themselves in mirrors. If they were good looking, they should learn how to be humble about their beauty. If they were ugly, they should learn to hide their shame and disgrace.

● The ancient Greeks used mirrors for medical purposes. Sick people visited temples to gaze into a mirror. If a healthy-looking reflection stared back, they were expected to get better. If the reflection was horrifying, death was soon to come.

GLOSSARY

accuse (uh-KYOOZ)—to say someone has done something wrong

chant (CHANT)—to say or sing a phrase repeatedly

disturb (diss-TURB)—to bother or annoy

encounter (en-KOUN-tur)—an unexpected or difficult meeting

grant (GRANT)—to agree to give or allow something

imprison (im-PRIZ-uhn)—to put someone into prison

inspiration (in-spihr-AY-shun)—something that influences or encourages someone to have an idea about something

legend (LEJ-uhnd)—a story handed down from earlier times

noblewoman (NOH-buhl-wuh-muhn)—a wealthy woman of high rank

origin (OR-uh-jinn)—where someone or something comes from

Protestant (PROT-uh-stuhnt)—Christian denomination separate from the Roman Catholic Church and Orthodox Church

rhyme (RIME)—a short poem

ritual (RICH-oo-uhl)—an act or series of acts that are always performed in the same way

warp (WORP)—twisted, curved, or bent out of shape

witchcraft (WICH-kraft)—the practice of magic, especially black magic

READ MORE

Andrus, Aubre. *Bloody Mary: Ghost of a Queen?* North Mankato, MN: Capstone Press, 2020.

Gagne, Tammy. *Famous Ghosts.* North Mankato, MN: Capstone Press, 2018.

Loh-Hagan, Virginia. *Bloody Mary.* Ann Arbor, MI: Cherry Lake Publishing, 2018.

INTERNET SITES

Britannica: Was Bloody Mary a Real Person?
britannica.com/story/was-bloody-mary-a-real-person

Haunted Rooms: The Bloody Mary Legend
hauntedrooms.co.uk/the-bloody-mary-legend

How Stuff Works: Where Did the Legend of Bloody Mary Come From?
people.howstuffworks.com/bloody-mary-legend.htm

ABOUT THE AUTHOR

Photo by Nancy Golden

Nel Yomtov is an award-winning author of children's nonfiction books and graphic novels. He specializes in writing about history, current events, biography, architecture, and military history. He has written numerous graphic novels for Capstone, including the recent *School Strike for Climate*, *Journeying to New Worlds: A Max Axiom Super Scientist Adventure*, and *Cher Ami: Heroic Carrier Pigeon of World War I*. In 2020 he self-published *Baseball 100*, an illustrated book featuring the 100 greatest players in baseball history. Nel lives in the New York City area.

ABOUT THE ILLUSTRATOR

Photo by M. Campidelli

Maurizio Campidelli is an Italian illustrator whose interest in art began after he broke his leg as a child. While spending months in bed, he read comic books and fell in love with their amazing adventures. Inspired by Marvel Comics of the 1970s, he began creating his own art and, after years of practice, eventually began working professionally for publishers and graphic design studios. In 2010, his artwork began appearing outside of Italy thanks to Advocate Art. Today, Maurizio lives in Rimini, Italy. When he's not drawing, he loves spending time on the beach, running and biking on the boardwalk, and watching Italian sunsets. If it's raining, watching movies and TV series is his favorite pastime.